Guideposts for
the United States Military
in the Twenty-first Century

Symposium Proceedings

September 16–17, 1999

Bolling Air Force Base,

Washington, D. C.

co-sponsored by the

Air Force Historical Foundation

and the

Office of the Air Force Historian

with the support of

The McCormick Tribune Foundation

Jacob Neufeld
Editor

Air Force History and Museums Program
2000

Library of Congress Cataloging-in-Publication Data

Guideposts for the United States military in the twenty-first century: symposium proceedings, September 16–17, 1999, Bolling Air Force Base, Washington, D.C./ co-sponsored by the Air Force Historical Foundation and the Office of the Air Force Historian, with the support of the McCormick Tribune Foundation; Jacob Neufeld, editor.
     p. cm.
    1. United States—Armed Forces—Congresses. 2. Military planning—United States—Congresses. 3. United States—Armed Forces—Forecasting—Congresses. I. Neufeld, Jacob. II. Air Force Historical Foundation. III. United States. Office of the Air Force Historian.

   UA23.G85 2000
   358.4'00973'0905--dc21   00-064304

Preface

Arguably, the rise of air power has been the most significant change in warfare during the twentieth century. While World War II demonstrated the tremendous effect and potential of air power, its proper application was misplaced during the Vietnam War. There, instead of adhering to the basic tenet of air power—employing it as an indivisible weapon—political and military leaders parceled out air power among various loosely connected campaigns. The indivisibility of air power theory also fell victim to doctrinal battles among the services. Fortunately, the United States military relearned the proper applications of air power during the Persian Gulf War and more recently confirmed it in Operation Allied Force, the American-led North Atlantic Treaty Organization (NATO) campaign over Kosovo. Kosovo demonstrated that the services had bridged the doctrinal divide and progressed toward doctrinal cohesion. Over the past thirty years, the application of air power has received greater emphasis with respect to its purpose, execution, and lower cost. The results have been most beneficial to the security and freedom of the United States and its friends..

Superior technology has enabled the United States to emphasize quality over quantity, talent over mass, firepower over manpower, and innovation over tradition. We have learned that the complacency of our successes threatens our technological superiority. We have also seen our weapons systems acquisition suffer from a ponderous, nonproductive process that emphasizes cost over value, administration over output, and the separation of operators from engineers. To defeat complacency and regain superiority in acquisition, the Department of Defense implemented a series of management reforms that supported continuous competition, concentrated research and development on high-leverage militarily unique technologies, and broke down the barriers between operators and engineers.

The accelerating hardware and software revolutions of the 1990s greatly impact the operational aspects of information management and information warfare. To make them integral elements of the same overall system will require cultural and structural changes as well as significant technology development. The new technology contributes knowledge and speed to the problems of warfare. It answers the basic questions: Where am I? Where are my subordinates? Where is the enemy? Our major difficulties are with information overload and information processing. In addition, because American business and commerce are so heavily dependent on computerized information processing, the nation is highly vulnerable to information warfare. Fortunately, our younger generation is fully up to these demands.

Another of the twentieth century's enduring lessons is that human performance is central to the outcome of battles. One indispensable element is professional military education (PME), which prepares personnel of all ranks for the increasing demands placed on military operations in both peace and war. PME fosters personal and professional growth and blazes the pathways to the future. The military service academies and the Reserve Officer Training Corps (ROTC) hold the key for training leaders by teaching military values and culture. Increasingly, the lure of attractive, non-military careers poses a serious challenge to military retention. If we are to retain the "best and the brightest" young men and women, it is essential to address the adverse effects of force reductions on morale and readiness, and to ensure that quality of life issues are being met. Suggested improvements include adjusting enlistment plans and offering beneficiaries of federal education grants and loans to substitute military service for repayment.

Since the end of the Cold War, a forward military presence has become vital to carrying out our national interest. This strategy enables the United States to transition instantly from peace to war. In today's world, with its new challenges, we need to be "right around the corner" of any potential hot spot. The new enemy is instability. As the United States faces new responsibilities with fewer forces and resources, our challenge in the twenty-first century will be to maintain our readiness to respond. To succeed, we must leverage technology with economics, business, politics, and diplomacy.

Among the threats to our national survival today, and which demand attention within the first five years of the twenty-first century, are geopolitical imperatives, homeland defense, and developing a national security strategy. We must ensure that the United States maintains its military predominance in space during the twenty-first century. Our national investment in space is literally and figuratively astronomical. For the United States Air Force, this fact poses both an opportunity and a challenge. Operation Allied Force illustrated our growing dependence on space assets. Moreover, because space operations are so expensive, the Air Force must cooperate with other services, agencies, and nations.

Contents

Reception Address

Photos and Illustrations

Guideposts for
the United States Military
in the Twenty-first Century

General W. Y. Smith is president of the Air Force Historical Foundation. He served for thirty-five years in the U.S. Air Force, rising from jet fighter pilot to four-star rank. Upon his retirement in 1983, he was selected as a Fellow at the Woodrow Wilson Center for International Scholars at the Smithsonian Institution. Subsequently, he became President of the Institute for Defense Analyses (IDA), a federally funded research and development center. He retired from that position in 1991. General Smith graduated from West Point and holds MA and Ph.D. degrees from Harvard University. He saw combat in the Korean conflict and was awarded the Silver Star, Distinguished Flying Cross, and the Purple Heart, among other decorations. His subsequent military assignments included a tour on the faculty at West Point and field assignments in the United States and Europe. He was assigned to the National Security Council staff at the White House under President Kennedy and served as military assistant to two secretaries of the Air Force and as assistant to three Chairmen of the Joint Chiefs of Staff. His two final military assignments were as Chief of Staff at Supreme Headquarters Allied Powers Europe (SHAPE) and Deputy Commander in Chief of the U.S. European Command.

Opening Remarks

Gen. W. Y. Smith, USAF (Ret.)

It is my pleasure to welcome you to the seventh biennial symposium sponsored by the Office of the Air Force Historian and the Air Force Historical Foundation. This year we have generous financial support from The McCormick Tribune Foundation, and we are very appreciative and grateful for that.

Over the years, we have encountered many reminders about the importance of history. In *The Tempest*, Shakespeare told us, "What is past is prologue." Lord Byron observed, "The best of prophets of the future is the past." And George Santayana said that "those who cannot remember the past are condemned to repeat it."

We at the Air Force Historical Foundation agree that history is important. We believe our mission is to make history more useful to the success of the United States Air Force and the other U.S. military services. We strive to do that without becoming "prisoners" of history.

More than two years ago, as we began planning for this symposium, there was great interest in the new millennium. A major question was how to meet this new millennium and mold it to serve our purposes. The chairman of the Joint Chiefs of Staff (JCS) put out his *Vision 2010* statement, an example of the thinking of the time. Subsequently, each of the services produced derivatives of that, so there were several explorations of how to deal with the new millennium and how to adjust it. Also in 1997, the possible impact of Y2K—the year 2000—on a wide range of human endeavors was coming into prominence and many serious individuals were beginning to think about how to meet the potential problems. At the Foundation we asked: "How can we combine our interest in history with our interest in the new millennium?" Our solution was to address the question: "What has the Twentieth Century taught the U.S. military that would or should be useful in the Twenty-first Century?" Having agreed to explore that possibility, our next challenge was how to identify the important lessons that have been learned.

Our approach was to ask past and present U.S. military leaders to share with the symposium attendees some thoughts and observations they considered important for the future. We organized six seminars and two special addresses to do that. As our program indicates, the topics to be covered are broad and far-reaching, but they are central to the future success of the U.S. military services.

Our speakers and panelists will first present their observations and then open the seminars to questions. There are two ways to ask questions. One is to write your questions on a card and hand it to junior officers, who will bring the cards to the podium. A second way is simply to raise your hand and have the speaker recognize you; you may ask your question from the floor.

Before we begin, I want to thank three people who have made this symposium possible. First is Lt. Col. Maynard "Bing" Binge, the executive director of the Foundation. He is dedicated, hard working, untiring, and unflappable. Ms. Sherrie Johnston is our lady-of-all trades. She, too, has shown that she is innovative, hard-working, flexible, and also untiring. We are very grateful to both of them. Finally, I wish to thank our conference chairman, Lt. Gen. Abbott C. Greenleaf. He came to our assistance when we really needed help and added an important dimension to the planning and to the execution of the symposium. We are very much indebted to him.

Part I

Larry D. Welch was born June 9, 1934, in Guymon, Oklahoma, and graduated from Liberal (Kansas) High School in 1952. He earned a BA degree in business administration from the University of Maryland and an MS degree in international relations from the George Washington University, Washington, D.C. He enlisted in the Kansas National Guard in October 1951, serving with the 161st Armored Field Artillery until he enlisted the U.S. Air Force. In November 1953, he entered the aviation cadet program and received his pilot wings and commission as a second lieutenant. General Welch served in tactical fighter units in Europe, the continental United States, and Alaska before his arrival in Vietnam where he flew combat missions in F–4Cs over North and South Vietnam and Laos. After completing the Armed Forces Staff College in July 1967, he was assigned to Headquarters U.S. Air Force, Washington, D. C., under the assistant chief of staff for studies and analysis. Upon graduation from the National War College in July 1972, he was assigned to Tactical Air Command (TAC), where he served in wing deputy commander for operations, vice commander and wing commander positions. The general is a command pilot with more than 6,500 flying hours. His military decorations and awards include the Defense Distinguished Service Medal with oak leaf cluster, Distinguished Service Medal with oak leaf cluster, Legion of Merit with oak leaf cluster. Distinguished Flying Cross, and several other medals. He was promoted to general August 1, 1984, and assumed the position of Chief of Staff, United States Air Force in July 1986. Subsequently, he became president of the Institute for Defense Analyses (IDA).

Combat Lessons of the Twentieth Century

Gen. Larry D. Welch, USAF (Ret.)

My assigned task this morning is to lead a seminar on the lessons of combat in the twentieth century. While I accept the assignment, the subject is bigger and broader than all of us, so you will understand if I focus most on the role of air power, which includes air and space power. To escape the taint of parochialism, I emphasize air power, which is more than Air Force. Air power is part of every service's business. In numbers of aircraft, the Army outclasses all; the Navy measures power projection in terms of manned or unmanned air power; and the air side of the Marine air-ground team continues to increase in importance. In addition, you will not be surprised that I will dwell more on the last half of the century. I share with many in this room the privilege of having served at a time when America's air power had matured to the point of realizing the potential long seen by visionaries. In my last assignment, I took the opportunity to read the oral histories of several individuals who formed that vision and who dedicated their lives to making it happen. And I served with a number of the latter-day leaders who made the right things happen. So, accepting the standard risk applied to most of us of remembering things that did not happen, I am significantly more secure in talking about the lessons of the second half of the century.

Combat lessons involve a complex, multidimensional set of issues. To frame those issues, I will carry three themes through my comments: (1) the knowledge about what to do with air power—purpose; (2) the capability of air power to carry out the purpose—execution; and (3) the cost of execution in the blood of airmen and the civilian victims of war.

This latter theme is increasingly important, as it strongly drives political willingness to use military power to support national interests. I spent most of the day yesterday with a group of business executives, academics, and senior retired government people reviewing a draft of our report, "Human Resources Strategy for the Department of Defense." The retired military there took exception to the first line of the draft, which stated that our military force is made up of the highest quality people in our history. One senior member suggested that we show our people the first ten minutes of the film *Saving Private Ryan* and ask how many would do that. That was not a pejorative comment about the courage and dedication of our modern soldiers, sailors, airmen, and marines. It was an expression of the difference in what we expect. By all of the measures I know, military

World War II bomber—the Boeing B–17 in flight.

air power has been on a dramatically rising curve—particularly over the past three decades—with more effective emphasis on purpose, execution, and lower costs in the blood of airmen and civilians. Even so, the potential of air power is such that we are just now in a takeoff position to move to the fuller potential of air power effectiveness. In a nutshell, we have long been on the right heading, and now we have the needed airspeed. To illustrate and discuss that set of claims, I will focus most on the lessons and results of the four most recent combat experiences: the failure of air power to meet expectations in the Vietnam War; the almost unconditional success of air power in the Gulf War; the last-minute save after months of misapplication in Bosnia; and, finally, the outcome of the use of air power in the conflict over Kosovo.

Using the three themes I have suggested, history seems to show that the application of air power in World War I and World War II was often characterized by confusion in purpose, uneven and often ineffective execution, and bloody results for airmen and civilian victims of war.

When we characterize the role of air power in World War I as providing information in support of the ground war, it sounds rather benign. Still, doing that and everything that went along with doing that turned out to be a risky business for airmen. According to Williamson Murray's research, the Royal Air Force (RAF) sent more than 1,400 pilots to France in the latter half of 1917. A year later, only 11 percent were fit for combat. The rest were killed, maimed, missing in action, or sent home with a variety of disabling conditions. On balance, the likelihood of surviving trench warfare was higher than the likelihood of surviving a tour as a combat aviator.

By the early 1920s, air power visionaries were fashioning a radically different view of the role of air power in future conflicts—the vision that air power would be primarily of strategic value, carrying the war quickly and decisively to the heart of the enemy's ability and will to sustain war—with the emphasis on the will to sustain. Although expectations about the ability of air power to affect an enemy's will to continue the conflict have consistently been optimistic, that does not suggest that advocates of the strategic impact of air power were wrong or that they expected too much from air power. To the contrary, I believe they expected too little. The underlying lessons of World War II seem to me to be three-fold: First, it is a far more reliable purpose to work on the enemy's ability to sustain the conflict than to count on destroying their will. We seem to return to that lesson again and again. Second, the versatility of air power impacts every aspect of warfare, from the close battle on the ground to deep strategic attack. And third, while the air war may seem far removed from the blood and grime of the ground war, it was, with few exceptions, still very bloody for everyone involved.

Again, according to Murray's research, in World War II, survival rates were higher for U.S. Marines in the island-to-island combat in the Pacific than among B–17 crewmembers, who were taking the strategic war to Germany. The U.S. strategic bombing statistics for 1943 to the end of the war in Europe were 51 percent killed in combat, 12 percent killed or maimed in operational accidents, and 12 percent held in German prisoner of war (POW) camps. Only 25 percent survived intact. Eventually, strategic attacks did succeed in grinding down the German *capability* to continue the war. But, I find little historical support for counting on destroying the enemy's *will*. While the strategic war continued to grind up both German targets and Allied aircrews, air power played a powerful role in tactical support of the ground war, and there were, indeed, some important lessons to be learned, especially the central lesson of North Africa: that the piecemeal application of tactical air power is doomed to failure and that concentration of effort works. Similarly, the lesson of the U.S. Third Army's drive across Europe emerged when the Ninth Air Force—operating on mission orders, not piecemeal target orders—proved that focused air power could have a powerful impact on the ground war.

Still, by the time of the Vietnam War, we seemed to have misplaced those lessons on purpose and execution. In my view, the Vietnam War marked a critical turning point for air power. Vietnam was not a single theater of war; it was a group of loosely connected campaigns with the services undergoing different experiences and producing different lessons.

For the U.S. Army, the Vietnam War provided some very hard lessons. It called into question the fighting doctrine and the preparation to execute the doctrine. It did great damage to the noncommissioned officer (NCO) corps and the company grade officer corps. One of the modern miracles of military leadership is that by the time of the Gulf War, the U.S. Army had reorganized, redirected, retrained, and reequipped itself to field the army we saw in Desert Storm—the most effective army the world has seen.

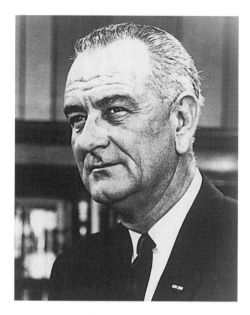

President Lyndon B. Johnson.

In contrast, the Vietnam War did little, if any, violence to the validity of air doctrine. Instead, the problem was that we lacked the equipment and preparation to underwrite the doctrine. Hence, subsequent generations of air power leaders—with the lessons of Vietnam burned into their souls—were committed to ensuring that U.S. air power would not fail again, and it has not, although the lessons of Vietnam may not be as bright and compelling as they were before the Gulf War. But then, it seems to be our nature to learn more from our failures than from our triumphs. From among the many highly relevant lessons for the future of air power from the Vietnam experience and extending through subsequent combat experiences, I chose four for discussion:

The first is that no military operation can be directed successfully from a distance. While I am a fervent believer in civilian control and the authority of the senior military leadership in Washington, their role is to establish the objectives, authorize the forces, set the rules of engagement, and provide the political top cover. Beyond that, no one removed from the battle space—no matter how brilliant and knowledgeable—can be immersed in the situation to the degree needed to make the right battle space decisions and to justify entrusting to them the lives of our combatants. I suggest that modern communications including video conferencing can lead senior leaders to believe otherwise, to the detriment of future combat operations.

When President Lyndon Johnson declared that not even an outhouse would be attacked in North Vietnam without his approval, that was not the declaration of an involved commander in chief. It was the declaration of a political leader who

McDonnell F–4C armed with six BLU–1B napalm bombs. The F–4 was the dominant fighter-bomber during the Vietnam War.

did not trust his military commanders. In contrast, years later, when President Ronald Reagan had given the guidance and approval for the operation in Grenada, an aide suggested a number of options for the President to observe the operation. The President turned to Gen. John Vessey and said, "Where will you be, Jack?" General Vessey said something like, "Mr. President, the troops have their orders. They know what to do. If they need something from us, they will ask. I will be home in bed." The President then told the aide, "If you need me, I will be upstairs," which meant asleep in his quarters. We saw a continuation of that attitude in the Gulf War. However, both the Bosnia and Kosovo operations were of a different character, with more complications.

The second lesson is that certain air power tasks demand the best capability that technology can support. While it is doubtless true that political restrictions and miscalculations played a role in the failure in Vietnam, the more relevant facts are that U.S. air power simply lacked the capability to underwrite long-standing doctrine. In eight years of operations over North Vietnam, with frequent interruptions, we never achieved general air superiority, and our operations were constantly driven by the air defenses. In the course of those eight years, the Air Force alone lost the equivalent of twenty tactical fighter wings. As to the air-to-ground business, while the environment made it virtually impossible to concentrate firepower on key mobile targets, such as the supply line to the South, we were also not very effective against fixed targets for at least two key reasons. One was that the lethality of individual weapons systems was so low that it required masses of airplanes for days at a time to do anything militarily useful against a militarily significant set of targets. The second was that the enemy owned the night. It was a time to regroup and repair. Consequently, the enemy's ability to absorb and repair damage was greater than our ability to inflict it.

Armed F–16Cs from the 363d Tactical Fighter Wing streak across the desert during the Gulf War, demonstrating U.S. air supremacy.

In contrast, during the Gulf War, we established air superiority within hours and air supremacy within days. In the ground attack role, a single aircraft on a single mission could destroy a militarily significant target, and night was the time of maximum advantage for much of Air Force tactical air and U.S. armored forces. Consequently, we were able to maintain a pace of highly lethal operations that overwhelmed the enemy from the outset and that allowed no recovery.

The third lesson is related to and repeated from the North African experience of World War II—piecemeal or gradual application of air power is doomed to failure. In Vietnam, there was not a single air campaign directed at the theater commander's priorities. Instead, there were at least six different air campaigns responding to the plans and purposes of six different authorities. Attacks against North Vietnam were directed and controlled by the Commander in Chief, Pacific (CINCPAC) and the Joint Chiefs of Staff (JCS). Attacks in Laos by Thirteenth Air Force reported to either CINCPAC or the Military Advisory Command, Vietnam (MACV), depending on the mission. In the South, Air Force operations were directed by Seventh Air Force, Navy operations from Dixie station, Marine operations in I Corps, Special Operations air reporting to who knows who, and Air America operations from the Central Intelligence Agency (CIA). It was a mess of the first order and the combat pilots knew it.

Again, contrast that to the Gulf War, where all air power not dedicated to defense of the fleet or the Marine air-ground bubble was directed in a single, highly focused, deadly campaign in support of the theater commander's objectives. Ironically, the roots of that are found in the Rapid Deployment Joint Task Force (RDJTF), established under Lt. Gen. P[aul] X. Kelley of the Marine Corps. I was General Kelley's air component commander. The primary mission focus of the RDJTF was to stop a Soviet invasion of Iran north of the Zagros Mountains.

The only hope of doing that was to focus every scrap of rapidly deployable air power against that invasion, in hopes of buying enough time to get ground forces in place.

I suspect that only a Marine could have established the rules and relationships that formed the Joint Forces Air Component Commander (JFACC) with authority over all Air Force, Navy, and Marine air, except that dedicated to fleet air defense and the Marine air-ground bubble. But the concept stuck and matured. Incidentally, to reinforce the well-known principle that where you sit is where you stand, in subsequent years, the Marine Corps's commandant, General Kelley, argued against a similar set of principles for Central Europe, although he eventually agreed to it.

The focused direction continued through to the conflict in Kosovo. However, for complex reasons, having to do with Coalition politics and miscalculation about the adversary, we reverted to gradualism for several weeks. It would not be unreasonable to believe that gradualism was significantly detrimental to the goal of protecting those who were the victims of that conflict.

The fourth lesson is that human performance plays the central role in the outcome of battles—air, land, or sea—regardless of the quality of weapons systems. We sent crews into combat in Vietnam that, by the time of the Gulf War, would not have been considered qualified to participate in a Red Flag training exercise at Nellis Air Force Base, Nevada, or a Strike University exercise at Fallon Naval Air Station, Nevada. The conventional wisdom was that if an aircrew could survive the first ten missions, there was a good chance they would become an effective combat crew. In contrast, in the Gulf War, we expected crews to be completely effective on their first combat mission, at night and against defenses potentially an order of magnitude more formidable. We expected it because of high training standards, and the crews delivered.

Again, the standards for human performance have continued to match the capabilities of the weapons systems, and we saw combat crew performance in the conflict in Kosovo that certainly met every expectation. I saw some combat film of an electro-optical (EO) guided weapon attack that graphically illustrates that performance. The target was a surface-to-air (SAM) missile site. As the weapon approached the target, the crew realized that a church was inside the circle of likely heavy collateral damage. In the few seconds available, the crew analyzed the situation, reset the aimpoint away from the church, and destroyed the SAM site without damaging the church.

Related to those four lessons from Vietnam through Kosovo, and reaching back to World War II and the Korean War, are four basic enablers that underwrite the enormous increase in air power capability and that have important implications for future development. They are: (1) the increased lethality per weapon that comes with precision-guided weapons; (2) the ability to maintain an intense operational pace around the clock thanks to night and all-weather capabilities; (3) training quality that enables the human capability to exploit weapons systems capabilities; and (4) command, control, and information to direct that capability at the right set of targets at the right time.

An A–10 in flight over the Balkans during Operation Allied Force, the interdiction campaign against Serbian forces in Kosovo.

As to the implications of those lessons for the future, the bad news is that the secrets of success I have just suggested are not secrets at all. Many of them are both widely known and available. Precision weapons and night and all-weather systems are for sale at the world's arms bazaars as we speak. I can provide you with catalogs and price lists. As for information, there are plans over the next decade to launch some 1,700 communications and imaging satellites. Consequently, reasonably secure, reasonably jam resistant, wideband communications will be available to anyone who has the money to buy the service. Imagery with resolution, once available only from supersecret U.S. satellite systems, will be for sale to anyone with the means to buy the service. And competition will ensure that none of this will be all that expensive.

Still, the United States can have lasting advantages in exploiting the most dramatic changes in what drives the effective application of combat power. Until Desert Storm, the "drivers" were clearly response time and lethality. Low lethality per weapon meant that we had to mass air platforms to mass weapons on target complexes.Hence, many of us spent a major part of our professional lives learning how to mass forces and to package the support needed for massed forces to operate with acceptable effectiveness and survivability.

Now, with the high lethality per weapon, a single aircraft on a single sortie has a high probability of doing something militarily useful to a militarily significant target. That change has profound implications. To illustrate, in the Vietnam War, if, because of *lousy* information or *lousy* command judgment, we wasted a squadron's worth of F–4 capability for a week or so, it was "no big thing," since the wasted target destruction potential was insignificant. But today, if we waste a squadron's worth of F–117, F–15E, or F–18E/F effort for one hour, someone should face a court-martial. And aircraft losses were almost inherent in massing forces against a target complex day after day, and that was an accepted price. The odds were considered inevitable. That is not so today.

In Desert Storm, our forces faced an air defense system that, on paper at least, was more formidable than any air defense faced in Vietnam, but losses were small relative to expectations. The air defense equipment in Kosovo was far more capable than in Iraq, and the Serbian air defense system was far more competently manned and operated. Even so, with 35,000 total attack and support sorties, we lost only two aircraft and no aircrews to those defenses. Hence, with each conflict, the standard of performance gets ratcheted up, and the forces continue to meet the standards. Ratcheting up the expectations is appropriate because, as I suggested at the outset, we have not reached the pinnacle in clear purpose and ability to underwrite the purpose. I have already suggested that we are just at the takeoff point.

In the current national security strategy of shape, respond, and prepare, air power will increasingly be the enabler of national security operations, providing airlift, long-range air power, tactical air power, armed helicopters, and space-based systems. Whether the need is to shape the world environment, respond to challenges to U.S. and allied security, or prepare for the emergence of future challenges, there are two particularly pressing needs: strategic agility and decision superiority. Both are enablers and products of aerospace power, and both can provide lasting advantages for the United States over its adversaries.

Strategic agility provides the ability to shape the battle space before any adversary can set the conditions of the engagement, whether it is armed conflict or operations short of war. Strategic agility supports dominance in execution throughout the battle space or operational space—air, space, land, and sea. Inevitably, aerospace power will be the vital initial shaper, and the ability for early shaping has powerful warfighting and deterrence or responding and shaping influences.

Early response with aerospace power is limited only by priority and budget. If we decide that we want precise, accurate, first hour response and are willing to pay for it, we can have it with systems that operate through space. We already have first day response with long-range air power and massive first *week* response with combinations of long-range, land-based, and sea-based tactical air power—manned and unmanned. Our most challenging limitation in strategic agility is discrete control of events and influences where humans live—on the ground. For that we need air and ground forces and full spectrum options designed to provide a powerful first day response. We can have that; we have the technology. We know how to do it. But, it will take strong will, strong leadership, and a willingness to take higher near term risks to forge that capability.

There is no question that the nation needs that capability. It is a clear combat lesson of the last decade. For the smaller contingencies, such as Grenada, Panama, and Haiti, we had strategic agility. For Desert Shield, we were left with

Operations other than war dominated the last two decades of the twentieth century, as illustrated by this C–5 delivering supplies and troops in Port au Prince, Haiti.

only a very high-risk option—airborne units depending on tactical air effectiveness for survival, but without the means to match the perceived combat capability of the enemy ground forces. For Kosovo, we had no satisfactory full capability option. Air power was able to avert disaster and eventually drive out the Serb military forces, but at a very high cost to the civilian population and with yet to be determined long-term impacts.

There are clear opportunities for continuing orders of magnitude increases in capability to meet purposes. There is technology and need for more all-weather, high-precision attack. There is an emerging technology and a need to find targets under heavy foliage. There is a need, but not yet an emerging technology, to apply air power effectively against ground forces in urban areas. There is a need, but not yet a proven technology, for effective attacks against deeply buried targets, using nonnuclear weapons. Still, air power is rapidly moving towards the capability to destroy almost any target we can find.

That brings us to the greatest remaining potential multiplier of effectiveness—systems that provide decision superiority. That multiplier is the capability to provide information and access to information tools that give combat commanders the decision superiority needed to sustain a pace of operations and level of effectiveness that no adversary can hope to match. We are using John Boyd's formulation to stay inside the adversary's OODA loop. The concept to observe, orient, decide, and act was articulated by Col. John R. Boyd in the early 1970s, but did not become a reality until the early 1990s.

We saw the result of that kind of advantage in the Gulf War. However, that conflict was against an adversary who had very little understanding of this critically important dimension of modern warfare, an adversary whose warfighting experience consisted of massing waves of Iraqi people and armor against waves of Iranian people and armor. This was an adversary who had little conception of how powerfully and completely air power has hurled that model of warfare into the dustbin of history. In fact, modern air power, delivering lethal precision weapons, directed with high battle space awareness, can make the armored vehicle the most dangerous place to be on the battlefield. After experiencing this for a few days in the Gulf War, the common response of Iraqi soldiers under attack was to get as far away as possible from armored vehicles. Unfortunately, these lessons are not secrets and we have already seen the trends in Kosovo, where the Serbs exploited information, deception, and denial to significantly reduce the effectiveness of air operations against their ground forces.

Therefore, we have the need and the capability to move to new levels of decision superiority, to provide a level of battle space awareness that can truly empower commanders immersed in the combat situation at all levels. Precision weapons and platforms that can get those weapons to targets were the great enablers of underwriting long-standing air power doctrine. Information translated to decision superiority and rapid execution of the right decisions provide the next level of underwriting that doctrine.

Since the Vietnam War, air power—from all of the services—has moved from promise to fulfillment and has led the way to a level of force effectiveness imagined only by the visionaries. Today air power is in a takeoff position to contribute to and exploit strategic agility and decision superiority that can raise the air power contribution to new levels. The continuing task is to convert that vision to new and expanded realities.

Part II

Born in Memphis, Tennessee, Donald Gardner earned BS and MA degrees in history at Memphis State University. He was also a distinguished graduate of the Naval War College, having graduated from the Command and Staff College, and the Amphibious Warfare School. General Gardner enlisted in the United States Marine Corps Reserve in 1955, rising to the rank of sergeant. Commissioned in 1960, he commanded a company in the 3d Reconnaissance Battalion in Vietnam during 1966 and 1967. He returned to Vietnam in 1971 as the senior advisor to Tran Hung Dao 30, a naval operation designed to resupply operations in Cambodia. He served in many other assignments including ones in Bermuda and Europe. His other senior assignments included Deputy Chief of Staff for Requirements and Programs; Commanding General, Marine Corps Base, Camp Lejeune, North Carolina; Assistant Division Commander, 2d Marine Division; and Commanding General, 3d Marine Division. His last active duty assignment was as Commanding General, III Marine Expeditionary Force and Commanding General, Marine Corps bases, Japan. He retired from the Marine Corps in 1994, after almost forty years of distinguished service. General Gardner became the chief executive officer of the Marine Corps University Foundation in 1999. He has co-authored the Joint Military Operations Historical Collection.

The Education and Retention of Military Personnel

Maj. Gen. Donald R. Gardner, USMC (Ret.)

Our Marine Corps traditions connect us to a proud legacy of past achievements and serve as a bridge to future success. In order to meet the challenges of the future, Marines must possess a thorough understanding of the goals, values, and institutional objectives of our Corps. One of the ways this can happen is in the professional military education (PME) process. The process prepares personnel of all ranks in the active and reserve forces for the demands placed on them by contemporary military operations in peace and war, and on measures to retain them in the armed forces for extended careers.

In his *Commandant's Guidance*, Gen. James L. Jones, the thirty-second commandant, stated, "Our educational institutions are an essential element of follow-on training. During the educational process, Marines experience personal and professional growth that not only enhances their value to the Corps, but also increases their self-worth and productivity." We extend these opportunities to all Marines by capitalizing on advances in technology and the quality of our courses to increase the span of our professional military education system. With the recent changes to our distance learning programs, for example, we are reaching an ever-growing population, to the great benefit of the Corps. We will continue to build upon our success in this area, endeavoring to provide the advantages of PME to the greatest possible number of Marines throughout their careers. Further, we continue to emphasize the role of PME—whether resident or distance learning—in our promotion process.

In 1985, after a thorough review of the military education system, the Marine Corps began a series of changes designed to institutionalize the officer and enlisted PME programs. Over the next several years, PME structure and curriculum reviews were completed, outlining the professional development programs for the Marine Corps' noncommissioned officers (NCOs), staff noncommissioned officers (SNCOs), and officers. These reviews, which are still ongoing, resulted in the establishment of the Marine Corps University (MCU) in August 1989.

The Marine Corps University was established to reinforce the concept of PME as a mainstream part of every Marine's career. MCU is comprised of the NCO School, SNCO Academy and affiliated academics, The Basic School (TBS), Amphibious Warfare School (AWS), Command and Control Systems School (CCSS), Command and Staff College (CSC), The School of Advanced

"Marine Corps University."
(Photo courtesy of Research Center Archives.)

Warfighting (SAW), and the Marine Corps War College (MCWAR),.

The university provides a focal point for all PME programs and the continuum for PME in the Marine Corps. All resident and nonresident PME—from a corporal attending his or her first NCO school to a lieutenant colonel attending our senior service school, MCWAR—is the domain of the Marine Corps University.

PME is the lifelong study of the foundations of the military profession. The program is designed to equip Marines with the skills, confidence, understanding, and vision to exercise sound military judgment in battle. All officers, staff non-commissioned officers, and noncommissioned officers participate in this program.

The objectives of this program are: (1) to develop officers skilled in the employment of combat forces and the conduct of war; (2) to instill in these officers the skill and knowledge necessary to make sound decisions in progressively more demanding command and staff positions; (3) to improve the professional backgrounds and military education of officers, subsequently improving operational excellence of both single-service and joint military forces; and finally (4) to develop strategic thinkers and operational level warfighters. A discussion of the five PME levels for officers follows:

Pre-commissioning Level. Conducted by the service academies, Reserve Officer Training Corps (ROTC) units, and Officer Candidate School (OCS). OCS is located at Quantico, Virginia, and integrates its program with those of the other commissioning programs to meet the needs of the Marine Corps.

Primary and Career Level. Conducted at Quantico by TBS, AWS, and CCSS. These schools focus on developing proficiency in military specialties and the tactical employment of military units.

a. The Basic School (TBS) is a six-month-long primary course attended by all second lieutenants after commissioning. The course lays the foundation of officer basics prior to initial military occupational specialty training and assignment to the Fleet Marine Force (FMF).

b. The Amphibious Warfare School (AWS) is a nine-month-long career course provided to captains. It is designed to enhance the skills and knowledge needed to operate effectively on a Marine Air-Ground Task Force (MAGTF) staff or in a command billet as a captain or a major. AWS provides the first study of joint service operations.

c. The Command and Control Systems School (CCSS) is a ten-month-long AWS equivalent with a communications and information systems orientation that emphasizes command and control functions within the MAGTF.

Intermediate Level. Conducted at Quantico by the ten-month CSC course, and its follow-on advanced eleven-month course, the School of Advanced Warfighting, is designed to prepare majors for MAGTF, departmental, joint, and high-level service staff assignments. CSC provides its students phase I professional joint education (PJE).

Senior Level. Conducted at Quantico, MCWAR is a ten-month war college of advanced strategic studies that prepares graduates for follow-on assignment as members of the CSC faculty, and for subsequent senior command and staff responsibilities.

General Officer Level. Normally conducted within the Washington, D.C. area. Education at this level is inherently joint in nature. Its focus is on theater-level joint and multinational operations and highest levels of strategy. The National Defense University provides general officer education.

As an alumnus of all of these courses, I am certain that this military education framework enhanced my fitness for command and staff at the next rank. The Marine Corps University curriculum has evolved from one emulating the U.S. Army to one rooted in the Marine Corps' roles and missions, in both Naval Expeditionary Force and Joint Task Force operations. The university educates its officers in the professional skills needed to function on the contemporary battlefield and provides them with the knowledge necessary to place such operations within a larger national security context.

The adjunct faculty and the permanent faculty, both military and civilian, expose the students to extensive experience in relevant fields of study. These disciplines include military history, national security affairs, defense economics,

U.S. Marines board the SS *Mayaguez* during the 1975 action.

area studies, and law. It is a unique opportunity for the student to develop. I cannot imagine continuing one's career and not continuing to develop. Education is a neverending process.

Prominent Marines are alumni, including Maj. Clifton Cates, later commandant of the Marine Corps; Maj. Roy Geiger, later commanding general, III Marine Amphibious Corps and 10th Army on Okinawa; Lt. Col. O. P. Smith, commanding general, 1st Marine Division, Chosin Reservoir, Korea; and contemporary leaders like Generals A. M. Gray, Carl Mundy, Jr., and A. C. Zinni, now commander in chief of U.S. Central Command. My last school was the Joint Flag Officer Warfighting Course. I have fond memories of my class, which included Generals Hugh Shelton, Joseph Ralston, and Howell Estes.

Although students chosen for these courses come from every conceivable occupational specialty, background, and experience level, they all have one common desire—to get to know the classmates with whom they will spend the rest of their careers. Lifetime friendships that literally span the globe are forged in the classroom, on the sports field, and in the social settings. Gen. Roy Spiekermare, one of our Dutch classmates, went on to be the commandant of the Dutch Marine Corps, and there are other examples. This kind of bonding contributes significantly to one's growth and development. The camaraderie fostered is never forgotten in peace or war.

In recent years, there was a decline of PME. One needs only to study the devastating House Armed Services Committee report of the late 1980s. I attended the Naval War College, the finest institution of its kind. Regretfully, the Navy still resolutely refuses to send many of its officers to school. This is their loss and ours when their students are not present. Not long ago, the National Defense University seriously considered laying off their civilian faculty to purchase state-of-the-art computers. This suggests a disdain for serious military education. We can sometimes become anti-intellectual. For an elaboration of these thoughts, see Lt. Gen. Don Holder and Dr. Williamson Murray's article in the *Joint Force Quarterly* entitled "Professional Military Education in the Next Century."

Only the Marine Corps has upgraded its entire educational system with extra emphasis on making it more intellectual. Perhaps we had the most improvements to make, but I do not think so. The commandant's reading lists for all grades represent a lot of thought and produce Marines who can think. The books are available, and this is not lip service.

In closing, we have a first-rate school system that is getting better. It prepares future military leaders by providing them the most important foundation for any leader—a genuine understanding and love of history. With this understanding comes a perspective on the problems of the present. One can walk in the footsteps of Alexander the Great, Frederick the Great, Napoleon Bonaparte, Stonewall Jackson, Alexander Vandegrift, and Douglas MacArthur—learning something along the way. The quality of our schools and the understanding of history we impart there will determine the pathways to the future. Except for placing the best individuals in command, no other assignment is more important.

General Conaway was Chief of the National Guard Bureau, Washington, D.C., when he retired on December 1, 1993. As chief, he was responsible for the day-to-day operations of the National Guard Bureau, including supervision of the U.S. Army and Air Force Directorates, as well as advising the Joint Chiefs of Staff (JCS). John Conaway was born August 23, 1934, in Henderson, Kentucky. After graduating from Bosse High School in Evansville, Indiana, in 1952, he attended the University of Evansville and earned a BS degree in business administration in 1956. He continued graduate work both at the University of Louisville, School of Business and the University of Kentucky, School of Business. In 1975 he earned a master's degree in management and human relations from Webster College. The general was rated as a command pilot with more than 6,500 flying hours in over twenty-one different types of aircraft, ranging from the C–47 through the F–16. He was promoted to lieutenant general on March 1, 1990.

Retention: The Key to the Total Force

Lt. Gen. John B. Conaway, USAF (Ret.)

The recent trend by the Department of Defense (DoD) and Congress to trim benefits for military personnel acts as a major disincentive for retention. When compared to the situation in the civilian sector, these reductions in the quality of housing, pay, and medical care make military families feel that they are second-class citizens.

Some relief is in sight, however, as evidenced by the recent congressional passage of a 4.8 percent pay raise for the year 2000, followed by a similar increase for the following year. In addition, Congress has raised bonus money for many critical military specialties.

These incentives are vitally needed to retain key talented personnel in the United States Air Force, especially pilots and information technology individuals. The competition for personnel comes from the airlines, which are planning to hire more than 3,000 pilots annually through the first decade of the twenty-first century. That projection relates only to the plans of the major airlines. Similarly, the information technology field is fast approaching the same kind of critical shortage that occurs with pilots. For example, there are 30,000 unfilled information technology jobs in the Washington–Dulles corridor alone and many times that number nationwide.

Numerous large-scale studies have concluded that more money cannot solve the personnel retention problems for these specialties. Recent surveys by the Rand Corporation and others show that more money is a critical issue within only the Air Mobility Command.

On the other hand, in the highly mobile skills, for example aircrews, individuals would prefer greater stability in terms of deployments than they have today. That is why the Air Force has created the Aerospace Expeditionary Force (AEF) and Expeditionary Air Force (EAF). The USAF plans to create ten AEFs, with two of them on call for any given quarter every two and a half years or some similar plan. Today many young people have working spouses, and it is important to them to work together with their life's partner. Also, the AEF does a better job of incorporating the Air National Guard and Air Force Reserve into the rotations. The Guard and Reserve have always been available to help the Air Force in committed rotations, as happens in Panama, Alaska, Europe, and Southwest Asia. However, the main advantage of this arrangement is that it formalizes the cooperation for the Total Force.

C–130 during the operation in Panama.

The Air Force and, indeed, all of the services have experienced major problems with retention of their enlisted forces. Specifically, more than one-third of all enlistees in the DoD drop out before their enlistments are completed. The Air Force alone loses approximately 25 percent of its new enlistees before they complete basic training. Currently, the loss to the DoD is estimated to cost several billion dollars a year for all enlistees who do not complete their initial enlistments.

In the enlisted pay area, perhaps the most glaring problem relates to the erosion of the sergeants' pay. In past years, sergeants were paid at a rate that was seven times greater than that of the enlisted force, but that has now dropped down to only three times greater. While the pay of young airmen has increased, the sergeants' increases have not kept pace. This is a definite disincentive for a military career.

A possible solution to recruiting more outstanding young men and women might be to consider shorter enlistment tours for the enlisted force. Given the very fluid civilian job market and technology revolution in which we find ourselves, a three- or four-year enlistment for an eighteen-year-old today seems like a lifetime. We may want to look instead at a fifteen- to eighteen-month enlistment plan, followed by an equal amount of time in the Guard and Reserve with full Montgomery G.I. bill benefits after their service is completed. This would allow many more youngsters to serve who would otherwise never have enlisted for the longer period. Another benefit is that it would also allow the services to enlist a greater cross section of our population. Young people would have the opportunity to try the military and learn a skill. Moreover, the post-service education incentive may be as important as the short enlistment. Where would the funds come from? The cost of this education could easily be offset by the current cost of attrition in the DoD.

Consider that the federal government currently spends about $15 billion a year on loans and grants for college students. This represents a great benefit for millions of young Americans who may never have to serve their country. I advocate looking at a coordinated effort to give credit for repayment for those in this program who would perform military service.

The bottom line is that we need even greater integration among the Active forces, the Guard, and the Reserve, particularly today without the draft, to have a military presence balanced from throughout the nation. We need to work closer together to allow our young people to move between the Active, Guard, and Reserve forces, and perhaps even return easily to active duty service. Pay and post-service education benefits, and better quality of life, are most critical if the military services are to stay competitive with the booming private sector.

Born in New York and raised in the northeast, Dr. Schneider is a 1968 graduate of the U.S. Coast Guard Academy. He received his commission as an ensign in 1968 and served thirty years on both active and reserve duty, retiring in 1998 as a rear admiral. His military awards include the Coast Guard Distinguished Service Medal, Meritorious Service Medal, Commendation Medal, with gold star, a Navy Commendation Medal, and numerous campaign decorations for service in Vietnam. In 1976, upon leaving active duty, he joined the Coast Guard Reserve and became executive officer of the College of Marine Studies at the University of Delaware. From 1985 to 1992, he served in several top administrative positions at Drexel University, Philadelphia. He earned a master's degree in physical sciences from Wesleyan University and a doctorate in public policy from the University of Delaware. He has published articles and given frequent talks on research, productivity, financial systems, and total quality management. He is currently the president of Norwich University in Vermont.

The State of Military Education

Rear Adm. Richard W. Schneider, USCGR (Ret.)

It is my privilege to speak to you today concerning education and retention of military personnel. I want to share with you my perspective on this issue. First, I write as the President of Norwich University, one of the six senior military colleges in this republic. Founded in 1819, Norwich University was the first private military college of our nation, and it is the birthplace of the Reserve Officer Training Corps (ROTC). Norwich has the distinction of commissioning more Army officers than any college or university in the United States, except the United States Military Academy at West Point. It is appropriate for this audience because ROTC produces approximately 70 percent of all commissioned officers in the service of the United States. Our ROTC units, in partnership with many colleges and universities across the nation, form one of those strategic alliances that helps to connect and bond the citizens of this republic with our military. I am pleased to say that the ROTC students in our nation are doing incredibly well, receiving Standardized Aptitude Test (SAT) scores as high as any of the federal service academies. We are producing officers who have outstanding leadership skills and are academically prepared.

Second, I write from the perspective of a retired U.S. Coast Guard rear admiral. Prior to my retirement last year, I was the senior Coast Guard reservist. I served on active duty for nine years and as a reservist for twenty-one. In addition, I had the privilege of serving on the Reserve Officers Policy Board and I am now working closely with the State of Vermont Adjutant General. So, I have been able to see the close connection and cooperation between our active components, reserve, and guardsmen. I have also spent considerable time with students in pre-commissioning professional military education (PME). I have served on the faculty of the Coast Guard Academy, as instructor at the Coast Guard's Officer Candidate School (OCS), and for the past eight years as president of Norwich University.

Lastly, I write from the perspective of serving as a study advisor for the Center of Strategic and International Studies (CSIS), which is presently working on a major project on American military culture in the twenty-first century.

It is from these three perspectives—president of a military university, Coast Guard retired flag officer, and as a study advisor to CSIS—that I speak to you today. My talk is in three sections, the first dealing with education and ROTC

Future military leaders on parade. Norwich University ROTC cadets pass in review.

specifically, the preliminary draft results of the CSIS project on military culture in the twenty-first century, and, lastly, on the situation of recruitment and retention of my service in the United States Coast Guard.

Pre-Commissioning Professional Military Education

I am delighted to report to you today that ROTC is doing a fabulous job, and we are producing outstanding officers. The ROTC staff spends considerable time teaching the values and cultures of the U.S. military. Those values that bind us all together—honesty, integrity, and devotion to duty—have become the hallmarks of our military. America's schools and colleges do a wonderful job of educating our students, and the ROTC officers and noncommissioned officers (NCOs) do a fabulous job of teaching our military values, but they are spending more time teaching those values because the students need it. There is a different culture today than there was thirty-five years ago, when many of us in this audience were in ROTC or at federal service academies. I will try to thread together this thought of culture throughout my presentation. We cannot assume that students today think the same way that we did thirty-five years ago. In fact, seeing students every day is one of the real joys of being a university president. Students are optimistic, bright, and energetic. Certainly we have wonderful students at Norwich University. While our students at Norwich, at the other senior military colleges, and those students across the land who have ROTC scholarships are an incredible breed, they are set apart from the typical college students today. Many students are coming out of high school where the prevailing culture says that cheating is okay and where drinking and drug use are widespread. Many students arriving at colleges have much more personal baggage to carry than any of us ever would have thought when we were in college thirty years ago. Binge drinking, divorced parents, and personal experience with sexual assault are just a few of the severe problems with which our students have to cope. We do a great job of educating students in the applied sciences, mathematics, and engineering—all the disciplines that are so critical to the success of the U.S. military. What we need to do, however, is capture their hearts and inculcate them with the values of our military culture. We need soldiers and sailors who have the hearts of warriors, ready to engage an armed enemy and to fight and win, while also possessing the compassion, understanding, and judgment necessary for humanitarian services and operations other than war.

It is essential that we continue to strengthen military education. In fact, I would argue that the need for it has never been higher: both at the pre-commissioning stage and through the span of a commissioned officer's or NCO's career. One area that needs immediate attention, however, is the need to establish technological core competencies at each level. Technology will play an ever-increasing role in our responsibilities.

Overall, I believe that our ROTC programs and our service academies are producing the type of ethical leader and the educated individual whom we will need to see our services cross over into the next century. However, that will become increasingly harder to accomplish if our national culture continues to diverge from the military's code of honor, integrity, and devotion to duty. The students of today are not like the students of the 1940s. If one thinks back to the 1940s and 1950s, we knew that cheating was wrong, that telling the truth was expected, that we had to respect our elders, and that there was a high degree of patriotism and propensity to serve in the U.S. military. That simply is not the culture of today's eighteen-year-old. Our military culture, which has served us so well for the entire history of our republic, needs to be preserved if we are to remain the moral force for good in the world.

I have been privileged to serve as a study advisor for the CSIS project on the American Military Culture in the 21st Century. This is still a draft report and not yet released, but I wanted to share a small portion of it with you, to whet your appetite and ask you to keep your eyes open for this very important study. If I were assigning homework today, I would ask all of you, as my students, to read the CSIS study, dated March 1997, entitled *Professional Military Education: An Asset for Peace and Progress*. While I certainly do not agree with everything that is written in this work, I do think it is very important. Let me read just the six major headings of the section that deals with recommendations on culture.

(1) The strong foundation of relevant professional military values, still appropriate for the environment of the twenty-first century, exists in the force, but is deeply stressed and not wholly understood in society at large.

(2) Force reductions, high operational tempo, a wide variety of missions, and resource constraints at the operating level have exacted a toll on morale and readiness that may have long-term cultural impact.

(3) Although a strong foundation of relevant military values exists, there are ambiguities and conflicts among values that require clarification.

(4) Command, management, and leadership policies and skills require adjustment to meet twenty-first-century operational requirements.

(5) Quality and efficiency of joint operations have improved over the last decade. Still, harmonization among services for optimum force employment requires improvement.

(6) Reasonable expectations for quality of life for service members and their families are not being met.

Let me make two observations that I find most distressing and point to some of the cultural differences that have occurred over time. First, the study shows that a significant number of junior officers believe that the senior officers of our services are not telling the truth or representing their conditions openly to the executive branch and Congress. When I was commissioned thirty-one years ago, I would have never thought that of our senior officers; in fact, it was not even conceivable. Our junior officers, however, feel that in our own "can do" spirit, which is certainly a hallmark and tradition of all our services, that we are over-committing them and underresourcing them. Remember that this is the Internet generation. None of our services is meeting quotas for new recruits, and we are all experiencing significant retention problems. A culture of selfless service is not in the vocabulary of today's eighteen-year-old. In fact, a propensity to serve in today's military, as measured by a Department of Defense (DoD) survey of 10,000 high school juniors, is so low that it cannot be measured. When I became president of Norwich in 1992, approximately 8.7 percent of the high school juniors surveyed said they would consider serving in the military. Last year when the same survey was taken, the number that responded affirmatively to that question was so low that it was statistically insignificant.

So, where will these new sailors and soldiers come from, even if we can find them and attract them into the service? They will come from a culture very different from the one that any of us grew up in. At a recent flag conference with the commandant of the U.S. Coast Guard, I heard that we were experiencing the highest attrition of officers in the past twenty years, a rate of more than 8.7 percent. The stress indicators observed in our human resource area included increasing special needs cases; humanitarian reassignments; demand for work life prevention services; stress and depression; and risk of violence at home.

By the way, these situations are also increasing our human resources cost at a time when we have fewer dollars. Of course, we have put in place measures to help counteract the increased attrition, as well as the difficulty in recruiting, including increases in enlistment and reenlistment bonuses; college fund opportunities; specialty pay; recruiting personnel for both civilian and military; and training throughout and more frequent reassignments. All of these add to the cost of running the service.

Who is leaving the U.S. Coast Guard today? It is the fixed wing aviators, engineers, and our information technologists. These concerns are not unlike the things we have heard from our other speakers I will argue, too, that in the next three or four years, our information technology (IT) people will be just as scarce as our aviators. In fact, they may be even more expensive to train and to retain. The reasons our officers give for resigning are: nonmilitary careers provide geographic stability; opportunities for advanced education; and greater financial rewards and career opportunities in the private sector.

Robert Reich wrote an interesting book entitled The Company of the Future, in which he describes six glues that help civilian companies recruit and retain personnel. I believe that we can learn a lot from civilian companies about recruiting and retaining personnel. His six glues included: money, mission, learning, fun, pride, and balance.

I think the services have done a fabulous job on mission and pride. We have wonderful missions and should rightfully be very proud of our role in the service. We are having severe problems in the other areas, though, and the glue that holds together organizations: money, learning, fun, and balanced life are areas in which we are not doing well.

In the October 1999 issue of the Naval Institute Proceedings, Rear Adm. Jack Natter listed five reasons why surface warfare officers and submariners do not aspire to command, including:

Loss of job satisfaction

Self-inflicted pain, such as overemphasis on inspections

Micromanagement and zero defect mentality of superior officers

Lack of confidence in senior leaders

Erosion of benefits, especially quality of life for their dependents

It is interesting to note that while our servicemen are willing to suffer personal hardships themselves, they are not willing to see their families suffer personal hardships or erosion in their quality of life.

Recently at an exit interview, a Coast Guard junior officer wrote, "The economy is great, the stock market is great, I can do better even with the same salary in the private sector, with my own 401K [retirement plan], and I can certainly do better than the government can." What our officers are telling us is that they want advanced education, but they want it with the conditions that they choose. In addition, they want medical care under the conditions they choose, and they want to retire or at least have the sense that they can have a fulfilled twenty-year career and retire.

What can we do to correct some of these issues?

(1) It is important that leaders engage in strategic conversations, such as we are having today about the role of professional military education and issues that affect our recruiting and retention.

(2) Readiness measures need to be realistic. We must tell Congress when the resources are not adequate and let our people know that it is okay to say, "Sir, we are not ready to deploy."

(3) We need to stop the lie of doing more with less. Service people are voting with their feet and telling us they cannot do any more, especially with less.

(4) We need to balance work life options and recognize that many military families have two working spouses, that spouses have careers, and that the nature of the military family has fundamentally changed since the 1940s and 1950s.

(5) We still need to talk to our people and tell them the truth.

(6) Somehow we have to make it fun again. When our senior officers do not show that they are having a great time in the service, why should our O-3s stay in to make O-6 or O-7 or O-8, if we are not having fun? I believe that our senior officers are just as stressed out as are the junior officers and NCOs. They are not having fun any more; the surveys tell us that.

Mentoring has always been an essential ingredient for developing military leaders. I fondly remember two of my mentors who made a huge difference in my military career. I do not believe that mentoring is taking place today the way it was formerly. It is no wonder, since so many of our senior officers are under so much stress and overworked. The cars in the parking lots late at night at the Pentagon are not there because our senior officers are mentoring the junior officers.

Let me conclude with a test, and one that you need to answer quietly, deep within you. It is safe to say that this audience loves the U.S. military and, in particular, the U.S. Air Force. Most of us in this room are either active or retired military officers who love our country and our individual services. Would you recommend joining the United States military today to your son and daughter? If we do not recommend it, who will? I would argue that it is not likely that the high school guidance counselor or college professor, who might have marched with Jane Fonda to try to stop the war in Vietnam, will recommend military service to our youth. If we would not even recommend joining the military to our own sons and daughters, why should we believe that anyone else would? Particularly, why would those who were negatively disposed toward those in the military in the first place recommend military service to anyone?

If that is the situation, I would argue that we are in far worse shape than any of us realize. But I have great confidence in the young people today and am absolutely convinced that the newly commissioned second lieutenants and ensigns, graduating and being commissioned from Norwich University, are going to make outstanding leaders. Can they sustain and retain our military culture? And what of the troops and sailors they will lead in the ranks? Who will send them to us, and what will be their cultural experience? And how must we be ready for them?

Luncheon Address

As the Chief of Staff of the U.S. Air Force, Washington, D.C., General Ryan serves as the senior uniformed Air Force officer responsible for the organization, training, and equipage of 750,000 active duty, Guard, Reserve and civilian forces serving in the United States and overseas. With the other service chiefs on the Joint Chiefs of Staff, he functions as military advisor to the Secretary of Defense, National Security Council, and the President. Michael Ryan entered the Air Force after graduating from the U.S. Air Force Academy in 1965. He has commanded at the squadron, wing, numbered air force, and major command levels. He flew combat in Southeast Asia, logging 100 missions over North Vietnam. He also served in staff assignments at the major command level, Headquarters USAF, and the Joint Staff. As commander of the Sixteenth Air Force and Allied Air Forces Southern Europe in Italy, he directed the NATO air combat operations in Bosnia-Herzegovina. Before assuming his current position, the general commanded U.S. Air Forces in Europe and Allied Air Forces Central Europe, with headquarters at Ramstein Air Base, Germany.

High Stakes in the High Ground*

Gen. Michael E. Ryan, Chief of Staff, United States Air Force

> "Not too far into the 21st Century, the United States Air Force will be an *Air and Space Force*, and by the end of the first Quarter of the 21st Century, we will be a *Space and Air Force*."
> —Gen. Ronald R. Fogleman, Chief of Staff, USAF, January 8, 1997

It is a real pleasure to be with you today to discuss the lofty issue of aerospace integration. To any history-minded audience, it is important to consider where we have been before we consider where we are going. Certainly, in the twenty-first century we must ensure that the United States maintains military predominance in the aerospace domain.

Our nation, in both the public and the private sectors, has an ever-growing interest and investment in aerospace, and I expect the trend to continue. Consider the following: Aerospace sales in 1998 were phenomenal, with the Department of Defense (DoD) spending $42 billion, the National Aeronautics and Space Administration (NASA) $12 billion, and commercial sales amounting to $54 billion. Currently, space represents 25 percent of the aerospace industry's sales. The United States commands about one-third of the worldwide launch business. However, foreign players are emerging as growing competitors.

As a nation, our investment in space is truly astronomical. The government-wide spending on space last year equaled $30 billion, and that amount will be matched and surpassed by industry early in the twenty-first century. The Air Force represents a huge percentage of the DoD's aerospace capability. We provide the following:

90 percent of the space personnel and 82 percent of the fixed wing personnel;
85 percent of the space budget and 73 percent of the fixed wing budget;
86 percent of the space assets and 75 percent of the fixed wing assets; and
90 percent of the space infrastructure and 78 percent of the fixed wing infrastructure.

---

* A version of this address was delivered to the Air Force Association's Annual Space Convention in Los Angeles, California, on November 19, 1999.

Gen. John D. Ryan, Chief of Staff, August 1969–July 1973.

Every year, space systems and space operations account for a growing share of the United States Air Force budget—and it will continue to grow. That will be both an opportunity and a challenge for the Air Force.

The military implications of our evolving dependence on space-based military activities are momentous. As former chief of staff Gen. Thomas White said in 1957, "Whoever has the capability to control space will likewise possess the capability to exert control of the surface of the earth. We airmen, who fought to assure that the United States has the capability to control the air, are determined that the United States must win the capability to control space." I believe it is important for the Air Force to project into the twenty-first century, the domain in which we will have to operate—and the missions and the dynamics that domain will demand. It will not be easy or exact.

Even early aviation pioneers, in the opening decades of the twentieth century, would have had a difficult time predicting with great clarity the evolution of the aircraft to this point in the last few weeks of this century. However, many understood the implications of the aeronautical domain. Freed from the fetters of terrestrial friction, many saw the challenges, opportunities, and payoffs that atmospheric flight offered for both military and commercial innovators.

I submit that as the second half of the twentieth century has matured the air realm, the first half of this next century will mature our aerospace realm. The domain that it will encompass will extend from the surface of the Earth to the most distant satellite or spacecraft. There are those who would want to separate the aerospace domain. It is an oxymoron that they would want to work space in

F–16C armed with missiles during Operation Allied Force, March 1999.

a vacuum. But for me, that would be like separating the mountains from the valleys, or the oceans from the seas—it makes no sense militarily. For the foreseeable future, the aerospace realm will remain Earth-centric.

From a practical point of view, I believe the aerospace domain demands our military planning attention. As my father, Gen. John Ryan, said thirty years ago, when he was chief, "The aerospace domain is an expanding matrix for deterrence, and is the operational medium in which the Air Force is preeminent." Let me add that it must be preeminent. That is as true today as it was in 1970, when he said it at the Air Force Association's national convention.

For the Air Force, the aerospace domain reaches from airborne to apogee, and from liftoff to geosynchronous orbit. Until humankind does go extraterrestrial, until the commercial and military equities are beyond Earth's orbital sphere, the expanding matrix of the aerospace domain will increasingly influence not only the conditions of commerce, but the manner in which wars are fought.

I also believe, that from a conceptual standpoint in the military, we should think of the aerospace domain as a seamless volume, in which and from which we provide military capabilities in support of national security. "Space is a place, not a mission," and we must make tradeoffs as to where the best investment gives us the best capability to fight and win America's wars. We already provide intelligence, surveillance, reconnaissance, weather, navigation, and communications from and through space. The Air Force has invested heavily in the space segment of aerospace, where it makes military sense. Now and in the future, we will continue to fund and integrate those capabilities that contribute to military needs within the matrix, not within stovepipes.

Operation Allied Force, the recent conflict in the Balkans, illustrated our growing dependence on space-based assets. It also highlighted the substantial progress we have made in integrating our aerospace force. Connecting our

The B–2A Stealth bomber.

combat forces back to the United States with reach back is one of our challenges. During Allied Force, we took several steps to reduce the sensor-to-shooter time line—fusing intelligence, surveillance, and reconnaissance data into actionable knowledge for our commanders. Inside and outside our air operations centers, we merged aircraft data with overhead data to provide a near real-time combat picture to the air commander.

For the first time ever, we were able to almost instantly calculate the precise coordinates required for our Global Positioning System-guided munitions for targets that were identified with atmospheric unmanned aerial vehicle unmanned aerial vehicle (UAV) sensors. This real-time targeting capability uses the data fusion power of joint targeting workstations. In less than one minute, Predator video data could be combined with three-dimensional terrain data derived from national satellites, then linked via satellite and data link to the cockpits of combat aircraft flying into Kosovo and Serbia.

Our reliance on reach back to the United States for information and support increased our requirement for bandwidth five-fold since Operation Desert Storm. During Allied Force we connected forty different locations, in fifteen countries, using a variety of military and commercial terrestrial pipes and leases, interwoven with commercial and military satellite communications.

We installed 500 new Defense Switched Network (DSN) circuits and fifty new Secure Internet Protocol Router Networks (SIPRNET) and Non-Secure Internet Protocol Router Networks (NIPRNET) connections. We handled more

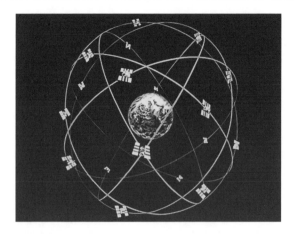

Model of the Global Positioning System of satellites that
coordinate all aspects of defense.

than 44,000 Spectrum requests—some terrestrial, some for atmospheric, and some for space systems. As you may know, these are very gnarly issues with our host countries.

Our U–2s flying over Kosovo and Serbia sent their raw data directly back to the United States through satellite communications. This reach back to Beale Air Force Base allowed us to keep linguists and imagery analysts at home station in California. They used their specialized equipment and collaborative intelligence links across the United States to turn that raw data into finished information that was disseminated back to theater air commanders.

Our advantage in space gave us a decisive edge in the battle space—it helped our targeting efforts with weather predictions, supplied much of our communications in and out of theater; guided our precision munitions with incredible accuracy; and much more.

The Air Force is not the only military service with an interest in space, just as we are not the only service that operates aircraft. However, we are the only military service that is involved over the full spectrum of aerospace capabilities, from inception to airborne and insertion. We will continue to be the service that integrates capabilities across the aerospace domain to assure we provide the best mix of synergistic capabilities, whether earthbound, airborne, or orbital.

It is not just the U.S. military that has become increasingly dependent on space. American industry is similarly invested and will continue to be so increasingly. That leads to another truism: space is expensive, especially if one is alone. That is why we in the Air Force must continue to engage in partnerships with industry, NASA, the National Reconnaissance Office (NRO), and other nations. As Defense Secretary William Cohen has said, "In the revolution in space, no one nation can afford to stand alone. So, while we will maintain the ability to act independently, we will seek the benefits of cooperative action whenever possible." A recent example is experimenting with our forward air controllers in the Balkans using commercial satellite telephone systems to phone back to our command and control nodes. The first test occurred in December 1998. The forward air controller dialed "911 Air Force" and received immediate close air support.

Those partnerships may take on various shapes and sizes. One partnership discussed in the *Wall Street Journal* last September described Pizza Hut's new "pie-in-the-sky" advertising strategy as the beginning of a new advertising space race. Pizza Hut had purchased the advertising rights to put a thirty-foot-high version of the company's new logo on a Russian Proton rocket—which is set to launch the international space station's living quarters sometime next year.

As we become increasingly more dependent on space-based systems, both militarily and commercially, we must be prepared to protect those vital equities in space. Neither the military nor the private sector can assume that our space-based capabilities will be buffered from intentional degradation or be immune from attack. We must develop the capabilities to know when our systems are under siege and to defend our space-based systems, as we do with those in the atmosphere or on Earth. We also must be able to deny potential enemies the use of their space capabilities and eventually to project power from space. The aerospace domain will be part of the battle space and must be integrated into how we fight. Air Force core competencies extend naturally throughout the aerospace domain. Aerospace superiority will always be job one for us. Information superiority is already dependent on space access. Rapid global mobility and attack; precision engagement; and, agile combat support have orbital applications too.

What we pursue in space for the military must be measured against its contribution toward fighting and winning the nation's wars. That is why we continue to fully integrate space activities into our day-to-day operations across the Air Force. Some of our major commands, centers, numbered air forces, and wings specialize in space operations. Space operators graduate from our weapons school. We have space experts imbedded throughout our warfighting organizations—they are integral members of our strategy, planning, and execution cells under our Air Force component commanders. In addition, they populate our staffs, giving expert advice on options and opportunities for the future.

NASA and other scientific organizations will continue to explore and push the aerospace frontier farther and farther out. The Air Force will continue to participate in that effort. Today we have nearly fifty air force officers—astronauts and engineers—supporting that effort on a full-time basis. However, we need to cycle them back into our force to enrich our reach for the future capabilities.

We are on a journey, combining evolving air and space competencies into a full spectrum aerospace force. In doing so, we will remain loyal to our core purpose as a military institution—to be a dominant fighting force, to guarantee the security of the United States in peace, and to bring victory in battle. Working together, we can make the Air Force stronger and provide a better defense for our nation and for the future generations.

Part III

General Carns is the president and executive director of the Center for International Political Economy (CIPE), a policy research firm located in New York City. The firm specializes in strategic assessment of international issues in the areas of international capital flows, international energy assessments, and Pacific Rim security. He has extensive experience in the leadership, direction, and management of complex organizations, having served as the Vice Chief of Staff, United States Air Force, from 1991 to 1994; as Director of the Joint Staff, Joint Chiefs of Staff, during the Persian Gulf War and the Panama Invasion (1989–1991); as Deputy Commander in Chief, U.S. Pacific Forces in the late 1980s; and as Commander of the Thirteenth Air Force, Republic of the Philippines, during the Philippine government crisis, 1986–1987. General Carns was a member of the first graduation class from the United States Air Force Academy in 1959. He also graduated from the Harvard Business School, with distinction, in 1967; and from the Royal College of Defence Studies, London, 1977. As a fighter pilot, he flew more than 6,400 hours and served the majority of his operational assignments overseas, four tours in Europe and four in the Pacific. He flew 200 combat missions in the F–4 Phantom II fighter in Southeast Asia during the Vietnam War and was awarded the Silver Star.

Advanced Weapon Systems and Technologies

Gen. Michael P. C. Carns, USAF (Ret.)

The purpose of this panel is to explore acquisition issues, certainly a topical matter for all services, the Air Force in particular, given the recent F–22 dustup. The general topic is advertised as technological assimilation and sustainment in the twentieth century. Since this is an experienced audience, there will be recognition of the impacts of prior decisions of the past four decades, but the main focus will be on our current situation, the resultant risks and vulnerabilities, as well as some thought as to "next moves, the big ideas"—not the new ideas— that need to be implemented.

General [W. Y.] Smith cited Santayana this morning: "those who cannot remember their history are condemned to repeat it." Nowhere is that more true than our experience over the past century in pursuing various procurement approaches. We hold a perspective that for the United States, national security is quality over quantity, talent over mass, firepower over manpower, and innovative force employment over more traditional approaches.

The enabler for such a philosophy has been technology, with the ability to honor excellence, to seek the best ideas, to push research, to expedite development, and to field decisive forces. In that pursuit, we have been both skillful and lucky. We have been skillful in enlisting America's best minds to work this challenge and lucky that no one else has been able to do it as well as we have. However, all is not well. The laurels of our victories are being threatened by the complacency of our success. From woefully low preparedness of the 1930s to the "do whatever it takes" attitude of the 1940s, we have since become mired in a dog's breakfast of various procurement approaches over the ensuing four decades. We have added debilitating layers of nonproductive process that yielded slower deliveries of force capability in an accelerating technological world. This decades-long trend that the Department of Defense (DoD) has followed fails to honor the very practices that this nation considers its economic foundation: entrepreneurial innovation, rapid technological insertion, and continuous competition.

We will explore this conundrum on this panel. We have three presenters. I will discuss our acquisition perspective, our market orientation, and the buyer-supplier relationships, suggesting how we might realign ourselves with our cultural

F–15C armed with the GBU–28 bomb during the Gulf War.

economic orientation for better defense outcomes. My remarks reflect several years of service on a Defense Science Board Task Force on acquisition reform, where many of the ideas discussed here originated.

Gen. Ron Yates will explore the care and feeding of the acquisition workforce, express some views on acquisition reform, explore the requirements establishment, and discuss approaches to sustainment through government and private sharing. Adm. Dick Riddell will then follow, exploring the impact of technology on naval missions, the challenge of emerging technology gaps, and some views on the resultant impacts. With that sketch of the agenda, let me lead off.

As members of the military, we understand that the national security challenge is very direct. When called to arms, we must succeed or die. Fortunately we are tested only periodically. When the fight is on, there is no more fruitful implementation of good ideas. We cut through traditional processes and pursue what it takes to get output. Recent examples are numerous, including about a three-week development period rather than three years, to get the GBU–28 bomb into the Gulf War and the incredible improvements in the sensor-to-shooter targeting process during the Kosovo operation—from days to minutes.

This is wonderful progress, but at the wrong time. The big question is: what is wrong with yesterday and today that should be fixed to improve tomorrow? The enormously ponderous acquisition process of today comes about for several reasons. Let me mention three that seem important. The first problem seems to be that the market perspective is wrong. The emphasis, the measure of acquisition merit, and thus the metric, is cost, not value. The management focus is on process, not output. Thus, in the ongoing F–22 dustup, the arguments of cost and "good enough" have dominated, while the issues of force decisiveness and battlefield dominance—output—have languished.

Next, the incentives are wrong. He who makes the investment—the parent service—does not reap the benefit or suffer the shortcomings of execution. He who

Deployment of troops and equipment depends partly on the
large-capacity C–141.

uses the investment—the CINC (commander in chief)—is singularly focused on
performance, while largely waving away the logistics problem. For example,
knowing the deployment distances and employment response times that most
CINCs face today, it is doubtful that they would have designed existing forces to be
as heavy as they are. Nor would they be likely to envision future forces that in some
cases are looking even heavier, like existing seventy-ton main battle tanks being
supported in the future by eighty-ton Crusaders. Another data point: the Army light
division of the 1980s was designed for 500 C–141 lifts. The kit for the twenty-four
Blackhawks deployed to Albania for Kosovo took 508 C–141 lifts, while the helicopters self-deployed.

From these two issues—perspective and incentives—comes the view that the
relationships are wrong. Even within the supplier community— the services—
the professional operator knows less and less about the trends of technology—
the art of the possible. The professional buyer is now increasingly separated from
his user as we stovepipe the acquisition corps. Said another way, unless and until
we have a smart buyer, a warfighter customer who understands technology and
what it can and could do, we risk widening the gap between the supplier and the
user. This is not an unrecognized problem, nor are there blinding new insights on
how to solve the growing dilemma. The business world runs by the same rules as
the military—compete successfully or die—but business is at war every day.
Success is highlighted, but death also litters the economic landscape with enter-
prises that failed to compete.

The military has taken closer notice, and we seem to understand the problem.
We do not lack for analysis and insight, but we are starved for action implemen-
tation. The current thrust for acquisition reform reaches back to the Packard
Commission in the mid-1980s. That commission also helped to spawn the

Goldwater-Nichols Reform Act of 1986. In 1993 the Section 800 panel recommended lists of law changes and the elimination of process. In 1994 Coopers and Lybrand presented a case that business pays an 18 percent premium cost to do business with DoD. One notable fix was MILSTANDARDS. Soon thereafter, Lockheed offered the DoD a 15 percent reduction in the final F–16 buy if they could use commercial accounting, but it was turned down. FASA (Federal Acquisition Streamlining Act), FAR (Federal Acquisition Regulation) updates, and FARA (Federal Acquisition Reform Act) followed within a year. But through all of this, old process was largely replaced by a different process, resulting in too much money continuing to be spent on input and not enough devoted to output.

With this brief sketch, let us cut to the chase. What should we do now? What few, simple but important, principles—"big ideas"—should be pursued to shift acquisition focus from process to output, from cost to value, thereby putting the best weaponry in the hands of the best fighting force in the world?

Let us consider five ideas. First, we must emphasize contracting needs, "value to the user," rather than cost to the government. By focusing on value, an expression of output, the amount of money that one is willing to pay is determined by means broader than its input costs. Cost analysis dwells on whether or not a supplier has correctly estimated his costs rather than what the product or service should cost—what it is worth. For example, for most people, the cost of a Rolls Royce is not worth it. You do not get enough value for your money compared to alternative choices. Today, the government's prescribed cost accounting overlays very costly processes that the competitive market has found unnecessary. With the proviso that a product market has sufficient competition, why not use existing commercial accounting practices to track cost *vis-à-vis* output performance, using CAIV (cost as an independent variable) as a tool to insure best value is being earned? This price-oriented strategy would focus DoD on value to the user rather than cost to the supplier. By not taking such an approach, the military is denied the best technology in today's accelerating technology market. For example, Hewlett Packard, a recognized leader in technological innovation, will not accept a government contract. We either buy off the shelf or go elsewhere. We lose.

Second, we should endorse the principle of continuous competition in acquisition. Just a decade ago, DoD enjoyed a robust defense marketplace, some ten major defense firms that competed to build the nation's weaponry. Consolidation has boiled down that number to three major aerospace firms: Boeing, Lockheed–Martin, and a struggling Northrop–Grumman. It no longer makes sense to conduct "winner take all" competitions, without also creating a real risk of future sole-source procurements. From "winner-loser" competitions, we need to move to "leader-follower" competitions. As we learned from the history of the advanced medium-range air-to-air missile (AMRAAM), the winner decided the design, but both finalists now produce it, with the procurement numbers competed from contract to contract based on value—price to the government. This approach has worked well with AMRAAM. This proven pilot concept now needs to go mainstream, with the Joint Strike Fighter (JSF), a sensible demonstration program.

Third, it makes sense to concentrate military research and development on the high-leverage military-unique technologies in those areas where there is no commercial equivalent application. Where there are commercial applications, we no longer lead the market. This is well illustrated in the information technologies industry where the commercial sector is determinant—the military is no longer a major player. Defense research emphasis needs to be focused on where we drive capability and fund it. One example of where change is needed is overhead sensing. This is rapidly becoming a ubiquitous commercial capability, as noted by General [Larry] Welch this morning. More than ten nations will have their own capability in the next ten years. Why not take the perspective that the military is in the niche business, pursuing that which is not otherwise commercially available, and turn over the overhead sensing "commodity requirements" to the commercial sector? This would facilitate U.S. industry, allowing defense to offer competitively priced overhead sensing commodity products, funnel precious DoD R&D (research and development) dollars to niche capabilities, and leverage the U.S. advantage. It is smart market behavior to avoid the commercial commodity business. Let competition regulate that market and insure a fair price. We should focus the military research, development, test, and evaluation (RDT&E) effort on developing unique technology niches, seizing advantage through leading-edge technology, remote sensing, ultra spectral detection, and so on.

Fourth, as alluded to earlier, we must break down the artificial barriers between acquisition and operations. This is one erroneous feature of the Goldwater–Nichols law. The acquisition corps concept is divorcing the user-combatant from the designer-tester. History tells us that this is a mistake. The operator is not honored in the acquisition channel; the acquisition officer is not honored in the operator channel. Each sees opportunity and promotion only within his own stovepipe, and it gets worse with seniority. The reality is that the user and developer are a fused set. There cannot be a smart buyer-user unless the buyer-user understands the market, its technology, its capability, and its future. Moreover, so long as the acquisition corps is a system outside of operations, it will keep to itself, nurture its young, promote its brightest, but live divorced from the purpose of providing the best for the user.

Fifth, there is the matter of output metrics. Measures of merit should focus on user-desired results, rather than process inputs. Output metrics, when established for each procurement, should help to satisfy one of four general principles:

(1) Acquiring superior forces at reasonable cost. This principle links directly to Joint Vision 2010, assuring dominant force capability.

(2) Choosing the right things to acquire. This principle requires that the article procured be tied to the nation's future strategic objectives, the envisioned threats and likely scenarios of that future, and the legacy of existing capability.

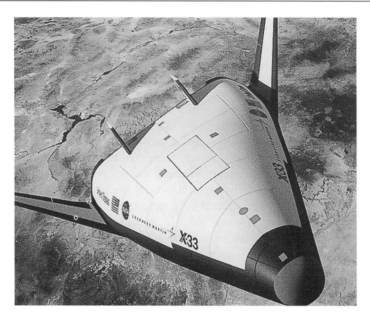

Artist's concept of the X–33 space plane.

(3) Doing things right to insure that the acquisition process acquires things of value, yet are affordable, effective, and efficient. Buying practices must expand commercial participation in the acquisition process to broaden the department's acquisition base and its access to developing technologies, and to expand competition.

(4) Maintaining the trust and confidence of the public. History tells us that Americans trust the competition process to deliver best value. They believe that competitive market forces help to assure fairness. They make value choices themselves every day of the week, from grocery purchases to new homes.

The Defense Department should pivot off this important cultural perspective and publicize that it also uses this approach to spend citizens' hard-earned tax dollars. It should encourage broader and continuous competition, establishing the value of things by making the user king, and using market forces to achieve better performance at lower cost.

In closing, let me loop back to my original opening remark where I said that, "Worst of all, we, DoD, have failed to honor the very practices that this nation considers its economic foundation." Defense should leverage what America does best: Trust America. Trust its ways. Trust its culture. Trust its economic system. The challenge is to make it work for defense in the same way that it serves our public at large. The United States has a culture for assimilating technology quickly into the marketplace and sustaining it to preserve market dominance.

The challenge for Defense is to embrace what America already does best—move to the entrepreneurial mainstream and shed our arcane procurement system. Act as a smart buyer in a market of continuous competition, reserving for ourselves those unique technological niches that add special leverage to an already technologically dynamic entrepreneurial culture.

That concludes my remarks. Let us now turn to Gen. Ron Yates. No one in retired mufti is better qualified to speak to the specifics of this issue. It was General Yates who served his four-star career as the last commander of Air Force Systems Command and the first commander of Air Force Materiel Command.

General Yates is an independent consultant to the aerospace industry. During his thirty-five years in the U.S. Air Force, he flew more than 5,000 hours in over fifty different types of aircraft. He has extensive experience in the acquisition business having served as program director of both F–15 and F–16 System Program Offices. He was also a test wing commander. He served as Air Force Director of Tactical Programs in the Pentagon, and as Deputy Assistant Secretary of the Air Force for Acquisition. He was the commander of both the Air Force Systems Command and the Air Force Materiel Command, where he was responsible for all Air Force research, development, acquisition policy, and logistics. He is a member of the Society of Experimental Test Pilots, a commissioner for the National Research Council Commission on Engineering and Technical Systems, a member of the Ballistic Missile Defense Office Advisory Group, the Board of Visitors of Carnegie Mellon University's Software Engineering Institute; and the Board of Directors of the U.S. Air Force Academy's Association of Graduates. He is a graduate of the U.S. Air Force Academy and holds a master's degree in systems management from the University of Southern California.

Acquisition and Sustainment

Gen. Ronald W. Yates, USAF (Ret.)

General Welch gave an excellent keynote address for us to talk about acquisition and sustainment. He started talking about his era, Vietnam, which was also my era and Mike Carns's era. In addition, he talked about two things that we were not happy about in Vietnam—preparation and equipment. We came out of that conflict dedicated to changing both of those things, and we did. First, we changed the acquisition workforce because we realized that even if we had the right technology, we also needed the right people to nurture that technology and to manage the programs. We also concentrated on developing the hardware, especially introducing technology in the operating forces. My experience is that when you give operators new equipment, it takes time to refine the tactics. Generally, I have observed that technology leads refinement of tactics. Once you place new equipment in the field, it takes the operator a good five years or more to figure out how to use the technology optimally.

Having said that, my experience is that the operators absolutely work magic on the technology that they are given. They do more with it than any of us technologists ever dreamt possible. They make up for deficiencies that we inadvertently put in, or that we did not correct, or for which there is sometimes no economically feasible way to make corrections. The operators really perform magic with that, although it takes a while for them to absorb it. The reason is that absorbing new technology is a complex undertaking; frankly, operators cannot afford to be big risk takers.

I am going to talk about building a work force and developing technology. I also want to say something about sustainment, although Mike [Carns] has discussed the crux of it. I must admit that I am not happy about where we stand, nor am I encouraged about the future. Therefore, I am going to disclose a few things that disappoint me and about which I am not excited, especially with the acquisition workforce.

Lt. Gen. Benjamin Bellis, USAF (Ret.), lives near me in Colorado, and I see him frequently. Ben was assigned the task of creating the world's best fighter. When the Air Force chief of staff said, "Tell me what you need, and I'll give it to you," Bellis did not ask for so many more billion dollars or say that he needed to streamline anything, or to change any laws. All he wanted were 300 hand-picked people, and he wanted to pick them. Those 300 people then proceeded to build a fighter aircraft that we still regard as the best in the world. There has never been a fighter that stayed on top for more than three years. That illustrates the importance of the workforce. You can get all of the other programmatic factors right, but there are so many decisions to be made, and they are so complex and so varying, that if you do not have the right people, they will mess it up so fast it will make your head swim.

Running a major acquisition program is like herding sheep. If you pointed all of their black noses in one direction, fluffy tails facing you, and you looked away for five minutes, then looked back, you would see half of those noses pointed in one direction and half pointed in the other. Therefore, you need some sheepdogs with the herd. You need good people at all levels. If you do not have that, there is no hope. That is why I am despondent about the future.

In my time, we "grew" acquisition managers who had previous operational experience. The reason for that was because we needed a healthy tension between the using community and the acquisition community. It is just as Mike [Carns] has described. You need to have mutual respect, and we must do battle over requirements, not to tell the user what he needs to fight, that is not the issue. He knows what he needs to fight, and his acquisition counterpart cannot help him there. However, the process can help him to decide on a list of things he needs to fight that are important. We can help in deciding on the list of things that he needs to fight that will support him. Ultimately, we can help him build a better weapon system.

When I became the commander of the Air Force Systems Command, I set out to establish a career development path. The one thing I tried to reintroduce into the command was that our officers have an operational tour. That has now fallen by the wayside. The other thing that was important in my day was that we had a military chain of command. Now, some people may ask, "Wait a minute. Aren't you the one who dreamed up the Air Force Program Executive Officer (PEO) system?" That's right; I am. I will admit that I absolutely made a mistake. The mistake that I made was this. There are a couple of critical jobs in the acquisition field that should be headed predominantly by an acquisition officer. I am not suggesting 100 percent of the time, forever, but predominantly. One of those is the commander of Air Force Materiel Command, and the other is the military deputy to the assistant secretary of the Air Force for acquisition. We used to call the latter the deputy chief of staff for research and development (DCS/R&D). Of course, there were exceptions to what I have said. For example, [Lt. Gen. Robert D.] "Bob" Russ was a wonderful DCS/R&D.

At any rate, I was the last commander of the Air Force Materiel Command to have had any acquisition experience whatsoever. I was also the last deputy to the assistant secretary for acquisition to have had any acquisition background. I retired in 1995.

What has been the impact of all of this? Well, if one works in the acquisition field, one thing to consider is: "What lies ahead for me? Am I going to spend my entire career in the acquisition field only to see a fighter pilot, who was a great wing commander, be placed in charge of acquisition?" That's not right. It stunts the development of our acquisition people who aspire to those positions. They will leave the service and find employment on the outside. By the way, I can talk about fighter pilots because I am one.

Getting back to the PEO issue, it was a decision that I made with [John J.] "Jack" Welch. Things were different then. The military officers in acquisition reported to me. Although the assistant secretary endorsed their performance reports, I wrote them; and they knew that I wrote them. They knew that I rank ordered them. They did not work for a civilian. They worked for me.

The reality is this. Consider an acquisition officer who works for a boss who has been an operator. The operator will come into the job for a period of, say, eighteen months, and he has never heard of any of the acquisition people. They will never see him again. Will the operator or the civilian official look after the people's careers? I don't think so.

Under this system we are headed toward a ministry of defense attitude. Under that system, the acquisition people announce that they are not responsible for requirements. Conversely, the operators declare that they do not have to be involved in acquisition. Under that system, the operators throw the requirements over the "fence," and the acquisition folks throw back a weapons system. There is no interaction.

This is not what made us a great Air Force. When I was commander of the Air Force Systems Command, the French realized they were losing out in the world market. They came to see me four different times. I must have been saying the right things because each time someone a little higher ranking came back. Finally, I ended up going to Paris and spending a week over there. Their warfighters knew how to fight as well as our warfighters did. I told them that they were doing their requirements wrong. Today, that is exactly what we ourselves are doing. It is fundamental, and it is wrong.

Not long ago, I had a discussion with some fighter pilots. They said that they needed "this and that," and there was no room for any tradeoffs. I asked, "How many of you have flown C models?" They said, "Which C models?" I said, "It doesn't make any difference, just C models." They all had. Guess what that means? It means that we did not achieve all of the requirements in the A model. Because we did not get everything we wanted on the A model, we grew it into a C model.

If you try to cram everything you think you need into an A model, it will not be affordable. And if you do succeed, you will not get many planes. You probably will not get enough to leave a healthy legacy to grow into C models. It is a bad way to do acquisition. Who ever heard of a requirement that cannot be traded off? If the requirement is to go 600 miles, how much difference will 595 miles make?

The other factor is that you cannot leave it at the top level. For example, I recall a recent experience of command and control, where the using community never defined the GUI (graphic user interface). Then, after two years, when the system came out, the users looked at it and decided that they did not like it . Whose fault was that? Not the contractor's. Another great example is COTS

F–15C from the 1st Tactical Fighter Wing preparing for takeoff during Desert Storm.

(commercial off-the-shelf software). In Washington, you could not hear four sentences on any subject, including religion, which did not mention COTS. It became Washington's solution for everything. People failed to understand that nothing is as proprietary as COTS. Certainly, the Department of Defense, as a minority user of some software, is not going to influence Microsoft or anyone else to give them their proprietary data of COTS. If the owner decides to stop producing it tomorrow, you are on your own. I am not against COTS; I merely point out that it raises its own set of problems.

Total operating costs are another acquisition requirement. It is a great idea of exactly where we ought to be. On the Joint Strike Fighter, we had a unit fly away cost requirement with no total operating cost. If you were a contractor, how much money would you put into life cycle costs? That's right, nothing.

In acquisition reform, to borrow a line from Michael [Carns], we must go back to metrics management. We need to look at how things work before we make changes. Then, we should consider how things are after we have made some changes and assessed whether or not we are better off than we were before. We also must form a baseline for measuring progress. Again, to use the example of Ben Bellis's experience on the F–15, he signed a contract. Four years later he completed development and delivered the first F–15s to the Air Force. We have been working on the F–22 for almost twenty years. Is this better? It has been a long time since I have read about as many launch failures, satellite failures, and cost overruns as I do now.

The question is this: We used to know how to do weapons acquisition. What has gone wrong? We used to have some excellent models in our processes and in our work force. We had excellent models of how it was done. We must go back and look at those models once more. We should then be able to decide what to keep and what to throw out.

Admiral Riddell completed thirty-six years of active duty in the Navy in 1998, achieving the rank of rear admiral, upper half. As a nuclear submariner, he commanded the nuclear attack submarine USS *Nautilus*. He was also commander of Submarine Squadron One, commander of Submarine Group Nine, and served in a variety of Navy staff assignments. During his final three years in the Navy, he was simultaneously the director of the Navy's special access programs, in charge of the policy and budget for the Navy's test and evaluation programs, responsible for setting the requirements for the Navy's science and technology programs, and the Navy's representative to NATO and fifteen member nations for research and development matters. He joined the General Dynamics Corporation on October 15, 1998, as an Electric Boat employee. He is director of program development for the president of Electric Boat, where he assesses the feasibility of initiatives in the areas of special programs, mission analysis, advanced concepts, and technology development. He also assists both the president of Bath Iron Works and vice president for international planning on technology issues and marine group international marketing opportunities.

Navy Operations Changed by Technology

Rear Adm. Richard A. Riddell, USN (Ret.)

I am going to talk today about a group of new Navy missions. What is particularly interesting is that technology has literally caused these new missions, rather than technology modifying an existing mission. By taking on these new missions, the Navy is making a profound change—a change that I believe will be interesting for historians.

There are a series of continuing missions in the Navy, including sea control, strategic sealift, and strategic deterrence—like the missile submarines. One dramatic change for the Navy is that, at the end of the Cold War, we no longer have the Soviet Union, or Russia, as the single major foe. Instead, the Navy has been thrown into a number of contingency operations in littoral waters. What does this really mean? The significance is not just that the Navy will be driving around in shallow littoral waters. It means a lot more than that.

Consequently, Chief of Naval Operations Adm. Jay Johnson recently recognized the importance of these new missions and has stated that "The U.S. Navy will influence, directly and decisively, events ashore from the sea—anytime, anywhere." That is very significant. In the past, Navy operations stopped at the shoreline. Previous military strategy dealt with the naval flank and operations were conducted to prevent an enemy from using the naval flank to his advantage. Generally, however, the Navy did not have a role in what occurred on the shore. The difference today is that technology has given the Navy a major capability to influence operations ashore.

Let me cite several of the missions that the Navy is assuming as a function of technology. One significant mission is precision strike. The Navy can now strike at great ranges, hundreds of miles inland. Of course, this has always been within the capability of carrier aircraft, but we are now seeing Tomahawk missiles being used and a variety of other missiles being developed. Even more significant is the idea of long-range guns. Today, long-range guns are being tested that will reach some sixty miles inland, and the projectiles are very accurate because of built-in Global Positioning System (GPS) and inertial guidance. Moreover, the range of these projectiles is expected to extend to somewhere in the neighborhood of 200 miles. Precision strike, therefore, includes aircraft, missiles, and, soon, guns. It is a mission that is strongly technology driven.

As a second example, the Navy is working on a sea-based ballistic missile defense. The significance of this capability when it becomes operational is that

Nuclear-powered aircraft carrier USS *Enterprise*, shown here approaching
Naval Air Station, Alameda, California, during the Vietnam War, exemplifies
one of the Navy's major roles during the twentieth century.

in addition to providing an area-wide defense, the system will not only protect
the battle group. Rather, the protection will reach ashore to protect the Marines
or the Army or whatever allied forces are ashore. It will also protect the populace
of the country, or at least a huge portion of that country. Thus, the Navy will be
able to protect our allies and block a ballistic missile attack by the enemy. This
new capability will exert a very definite impact on what happens ashore.

Similarly, the Navy has worked for many years on battle group air defense,
which includes defensive systems for cruise missiles as well as aircraft. The Navy
has found that with fleet aircraft flying off carriers, they can look ashore for a
couple of hundred miles. With continued funding, and a few more years, this
system will become operational.

Another capability will be support of the land battle, in the form of support to
the Marine Corps. This new capability will go well beyond the traditional World
War II type of amphibious operations. In the future, not only will the Navy
deliver and retrieve the Marines, but the Navy will provide the gun fire support
with long-range, very accurate guns and missiles on ships. Instead of the Marines
carrying their artillery ashore, the firepower will come from ships. And instead

of Marines carrying all of their communications gear ashore, the major communications nodes can be on ships in nearby coastal waters. And instead of the Marines carrying all of their logistics with them, supplies will be transported "just in time" to the Marines from the ships.

All of these new capabilities will enable the Navy and Marine Corps to be much more effective in the coming decades. Still, there will be some real challenges in the technology area. If the Navy commits to another country that the fleet will provide ballistic missile defense air defense, precision strike, or send Marines ashore, the Navy cannot back away from the coastal littoral waters if "things get dicey." If the Navy goes in, it must stay. That is the difficult part of operating in the littorals. Unlike operations in the vast blue ocean, the littorals are a fairly small area, where ships must drive back and forth in predictable, repeatable patterns. These conditions can be very hazardous to Navy ships.

For example, there is the threat of enemy submarines. The Germans, the French, and others are building submarines with air independent propulsion systems that allow the submarines to operate at moderate speeds for up to thirty days without ever taking air into their diesel engines. These are very dangerous submarines because they have torpedo and missile capabilities that are formidable threats to our ships, and these diesel-electric submarines are becoming very quiet during operations.

Another problem in littoral waters is the threat of mines. Mines are difficult to find and difficult to kill. When I traveled internationally while on active duty, some foreign navies asked if the United States was interested in stealth mines. They suggested that they could build them for us. We do not need stealth mines, because current mines are so difficult to deal with. Cruise missiles are another very difficult problem. Cruise missiles coming off the beach or coming off small enemy craft pose a great danger for the fleet.

These and other technological problems will have to be overcome in much better ways than we are doing now if the Navy is going to assume the new missions and the associated extended operations close to the shore.

Adding to the technological challenge of these new missions are other technologies that require improvement. Surveillance and reconnaissance capabilities need improvement. The Navy is developing much more capability for putting "metal" on the beach than in finding exactly where on the beach the metal should go. Plus, improvements are required in the communication capabilities needed to handle the greatly expanded surveillance and reconnaissance.

Another continuing technological challenge involves Marines going into an urban area. Urban warfare makes war uglier. And of course, the defenses or the counters to nuclear, chemical, and biological warfare are very difficult.

In summary, technology is changing the very nature of naval warfare. The Navy and Marine Corps are getting significant new capabilities for waging war. But technology is making the playing field more difficult and, in some cases, very ugly. This is history in action.

Part IV

Admiral Lopez was born on January 20, 1940, in Powellton, West Virginia. He enlisted in the Navy in 1959 and entered Officer Candidate School in August 1964. In December 1964 he graduated and was discharged for the convenience of the government to accept a commission as an ensign. Admiral Lopez held many positions of ever-increasing importance, including Commander, River Assault Division 153; Commander, Destroyer Squadron 32; Executive Assistant to the Vice Chief of Naval Operations; and Senior Military Assistant to the Secretary of Defense. His last command before retirement was Commander in Chief, U.S. Naval Forces Europe. He was promoted to admiral on July 15, 1996. Admiral Lopez was awarded the Defense Distinguished Service Medal, Distinguished Service Medal, the Legion of Merit with two gold stars, and twenty other medals of lesser rank. His education includes a BA in international relations and an MS in management. He is also a graduate of the Armed Forces Staff College.

Forward Presence, Forward Engagement

Adm. Thomas J. Lopez, USN (Ret.)

As I look at what we are supposed to talk about, "operations other than traditional use of military forces," and I have to think about the twenty-first century, it seems rather easy because the Cold War is over. I want to address today's world, the future, and the need for strategy. I believe that without a strategy it is impossible to draft requirements. You need not have watched CNN to know that the military has been very busy lately. It tells us that the world has changed.

In EUCOM [European Command], where Jim [Gen. James Jamerson] and I served, we have responded to thirteen crises in Europe and Africa since 1997. We were in Bosnia, in Sierra Leone, Albania, and Zaire; from A to Z. We completed operations there and simply stabilized situations by only our presence. The word *presence* has great meaning for me, and I believe for all our armed forces in the future.

We were not just there; we were also in the Caribbean and elsewhere, ready to transition instantly. That is another key word, the ability to *transition* almost instantly from peace to crises or war. The Air Force chief of staff, General Ryan, mentioned the need to be expeditionary and to transition. Our forces today are just as prepared as they ever were, except that they have been downsized radically. They are forward deployed and forward engaged, and they are one of our most effective weapons in the diplomatic arsenal. That is important, too.

Let me talk about the military's impact on diplomacy and politics, and how we respond to the global economy. Today's military is postured overseas. In most cases, if we are not where we need to be, we are right around the corner. But it is a new world, with new challenges. Those challenges are not as clearly defined as they once were in the Cold War era. I often tell audiences that for me history stopped in 1991. It then started off in a new direction, took a right turn, and accelerated.

Basically, "the train has left the station." If we do not have a strategy with which to deal in today's world, we are sure to fail. And we will fail not so much for us, but for our grandchildren. There is a new enemy, although the focus is not entirely clear. The new enemy is *instability*. Some of you, like me, probably miss the Cold War because it was easy. We knew who the enemy was, or certainly the potential enemy. We knew what the military's role was; it was very well defined. We knew who we had to fight, where, and how. Where we once had enormous resources, we are now down about 40 percent in force structure across the board. That is true whether it is the Army, Air Force, Navy, or Marine Corps.

U.S. Navy F–14 Tomcat in flight.

For example, the U.S. Navy is still the most powerful in the world. But it is smaller than it was in 1938, and there were some things that happened in 1940. We have to think about that. How do we best use our military to deal with the new enemy—instability—in today's world? There is more turmoil everywhere you look, and there is more to do. As the commander in chief (CINC) of Allied Forces Southern Europe, my command was expected to engage in more than forty countries. When you added in my Navy responsibility as CINC of the U.S. Navy Forces in Europe, that number went up to more than 100 countries.

We cannot do all of that with 40 percent fewer forces. We must make some hard choices. We must use intelligence in a different way. We must do predicative analysis to help make the hard choices. In addition, we must consider economics and politics, because the world is different.

Ultimately, the task is to prevent crisis and war. That is what it is all about. We only fight in a protracted war about once in every twenty years. During the other nineteen, we ought to spend our time productively, trying to prevent that twentieth year or all the skirmishes in between. If one looks around at what we have done since 1991, we have done a lot of that.

One thing that we can do is to obey the tenets of the national security strategy that shapes the environment; and we can selectively shape that environment. I use the word *selectively* advisedly because one has to make a hard choice before one can select what one wishes to shape. Now, shape means different things to different CINCs, and so does the environment. One must have the right strategy or the right forces to do the right thing—to shape the environment to prevent war. I am sure all of you agree that maintaining peace is a lot cheaper than fighting wars, not just in dollars, but in the costs that you cannot calculate, like human life.

I tell a lot of audiences, particularly civilian audiences, that I do not want my grandchildren to have to join the United States Navy. I would like them to *choose* to join the United States Navy, not to *have to* in order to protect American values. I know that without the right kind of U.S. military across the board that the choice will disappear.

Our allies face a different set of challenges. The war in Bosnia and Herzegovina forced Europe and NATO to confront the end of the Cold War and a new kind of strategic challenge to the Western Alliance. The new enemy, as I said earlier, became instability. It was that instability that thrust the North Atlantic Treaty Organization (NATO) and NATO forces into the forefront of the alliance's emerging strategic concept. NATO's horizons broadened. They actually were forced to broaden, I contend. It was fortunate, in some ways, because NATO can now be a catalyst for positive influence, not just a reactive organization ready to fight some global World War III.

NATO's operations in Bosnia demonstrated our ability to work in concert, side by side, with non-NATO nations of the European Union (EU). The EU's participation in Balkan operations reaffirmed the importance of military alliances and coalitions in ensuring stability during an era which combines increasing tensions and military downsizing.

When I commanded IFOR (Implementation Force) in 1996, thirty-six nations were stationed in Bosnia, including sixteen from NATO. The other twenty were non-NATO nations, and it all worked. I believe that example portends the direction for the twenty-first century, one that will demand coalitions and alliances. There will be no nation or no military that can go it alone, politically or militarily.

Just as our political and military leaders work and prepare for an expanded NATO, they are doing that with a growing consensus that the Southern Region (where I served) and its periphery have emerged from the Cold War as the arena of NATO's most serious challenges.

But in order to comprehend that environment, or that challenge, one must understand today's world. The Southern Region of Europe, I contend, is more and more complex and perhaps one of the most difficult in the world. The difficulty lies in the combination of geography, culture, political difficulties, economic issues, military issues, and much more.

In the Navy hat that I wore, I had to look from the Baltics all the way down around the tip of South Africa, and to the waters of the Black Sea. In NATO, the role was expanded to the places that I really never thought about in my previous life, Azerbaijan, Pakistan, Turkistan, the Caspian Sea—part of the area of responsibility.

All of those places, I believe, need to be influenced by the western system of liberal market economics and democracy. Since we cannot do it all, we must make difficult choices. We must influence as many countries as possible. But which ones? What's the strategy? The question is, how do you do that with a

U.S. Airmen from the 4100th Group (Provisional), operating as members of the Implementation Force (IFOR), help load a Swedish C–130 at Tuzla Air Base, Bosnia–Herzegovina.

declining budget and smaller force structure? Well, eight years after the end of the Cold War, we are somehow expected to deal with three times as many countries as before. Even when you whittle down the hard choices, it is still three times as large. The Cold War was easier—there was a clear focus and a well-defined policy. In today's world, everything is in turmoil and instability. You have to understand the factors that lead to instability, as you look at a country like Turkey, which I think is absolutely central not only to NATO's future but the United States' future. Similarly, we must look at stability in the Middle East, Africa, and the Transcaucasian region.

Political and economic factors are tied up in regional conflicts in some of those countries. Take the Transcaucasian region, for example. There are Azerbaijan, Chechnya, and the northwest corner of Georgia. Turkey itself has the Kurdish problem, as do Iraq and Iran. Jordan is relatively stable, but who knows what will happen, with King Hussein dead. In Syria and Israel, with all of the instability caused by religious and political extremism, demographic issues, like high birth rates, refugee movements, illegal immigration, military capabilities and intentions, including the availability of nuclear, biological, and chemical weapons of mass destruction, and ballistic missiles to carry them—some as far as European cities. The area is divided into the haves and have-nots in strategic resources, including the availability of oil and gas, but more importantly, something we do not think of normally—water. Those of you who watch that region know that Turkey and Syria could have a serious crisis or perhaps conflict just over water.

To counterbalance instability, the new Europe has become a constantly evolving landscape of interconnected political, military, and economic organizations and unions, such as the European Union, the European Free Trade Association, the Euro-Atlantic Partnership Council, the Organization for Security Cooperation, and, of course, NATO. I bring this up is because it is a very complicated organizational arena in which to operate if you are the military. The Cold War experience does not really help much because there are overlapping economic, political, and security organizations that are meant to balance the region but do not.

When I was in Germany recently talking on this subject, a German professor came up and asked how closely I had watched North Africa. He said that he had done some statistical work and found that the average age in 2005 in North Africa would be under eighteen. The average age in 2005 in Western Europe will be forty-three plus. You can imagine what sort of trouble that forecasts.

Religious, political, and economic extremism will be very attractive to the young and unemployed, a recipe for turmoil and future instability. One of the statistics that I saw was that about 25 percent of the gross domestic product of the entire continent of Africa would be lost before 2010 due only to AIDS [A(cquired) I(mmune) D(eficiency) S(yndrome)].

So, how do you make these hard choices? Some of the lessons I learned in Bosnia and through research by my staffs in NATO and the United States were to develop a vision and a strategy for the future of the Southern Region. I felt that we had to promote stability using every tool possible. In my view, the key tool was forward engagement. To be forward engaged, we must have a strategy of partnership with our business and economic interests, in concert with political and diplomatic priorities. The world is not simple any more. One cannot influence events if one is not there, wherever there is. And one cannot prevent war unless one is there. One cannot react to crises unless one is there. It is very basic, but it is absolutely central, whether in Europe, the Far East, or wherever. Every ally and the United States in particular, as the greatest nation on earth, has to be proactive, has to be there.

Of course, the military and this nation cannot forget the fundamentals. We must maintain defensive capabilities for our varied responsibility. We must be proactive in the sense of adapting to the changing environment. We must have crisis management skills and be ready to perform new missions or support operations. The previous panel talked about being light and fast. I would add to that mobility and flexibility. Because when you have 40 percent less force structure, you must be ready to move.

In conclusion, we must maintain our readiness to respond. That is the challenge for our nation and our allies in the twenty-first century. We have to take advantage of the opportunities we have in order to help ensure environmental stability, democracy, free enterprise, and prosperity in this coming century—all those things that we now take for granted. Also, we must leverage technology and be partners with economics, business, politics, and diplomacy. The strategy of shaping the environment through forward presence and forward engagement will position our forces so that they are best prepared to meet any challenge and act decisively. That is the key. While it would be naive for us to think that there will not be larger conflicts, it would also be naive to think that we cannot prevent some of them or at least minimize them.

Reception Address

General Ralston is the Vice Chairman of the Joint Chiefs of Staff (JCS), the Pentagon, Washington, D.C. As the vice chairman, the general presides over the Joint Requirements Oversight Council; is vice chairman of the Defense Acquisition Board; serves as a member of the National Security Council Deputies Committee, and of the Nuclear Weapons Council. Joseph Ralston entered the Air Force in 1965 through the Reserve Officer Training Corps (ROTC) program. His career includes operational command at squadron, wing, numbered air force, major command, and a variety of senior staff and management positions at every level of the Air Force. He has been closely involved with building the U.S. Air Force of the twenty-first century, holding a variety of positions related to the requirements and acquisition process. Prior to assuming his current position, he was commander of Air Combat Command, with headquarters at Langley Air Force Base, Virginia. He is a command pilot with more than 2,500 flying hours, including 147 combat missions over Laos and North Vietnam.

Air Power Perspective

Gen. Joseph W. Ralston, USAF, Vice Chairman, Joint Chiefs of Staff

Tonight, as I offer some thoughts on air power, I know that when those of us gathered here talk about air power, our only differences are differences of perspective. Long before I was Vice Chairman of the Joint Chiefs of Staff, I had come to the realization that air power, regardless of the service or services involved in its application, was still air power. The difference between an aviator who flies in the Marine Corps, Army, Navy, or Air Force is one of perspective. It could be a service perspective or personal perspective. It could be the perspective of one hardened in combat or one toughened in training. It could be the perspective of one who navigates on jetways or one who navigates on polar orbits. Nevertheless, it is perspective.

Having been in many battles—some lethal and some not so lethal—I am not sure I have ever gotten used to it. However, such experiences taught me to take my cues from the great air power thinkers. For instance, early on I studied Air Marshal Sir Hugh Trenchard's air control theory, which as you all know is the historical basis for today's no-fly zones. At the heart of his theory is the belief that air power is indivisible. This notion had its genesis in World War I, when pioneers like Trenchard and General Billy Mitchell began exploring the airplane's potential.

During the interwar years, doctrinal battles erupted among airmen, and the indivisibility concept went underground until it resurfaced in the early 1950s. In 1951, the then-Chief of Staff Hoyt Vandenberg wrote, "Air power is indivisible. We don't speak of a 'strategic' or a 'tactical' Army or Navy, yet those terms are applied to the Air Force."

At the time, a battle was being fought for the heart and soul of the Air Force, and political and intellectual forces were staking their claims and choosing sides. General Vandenberg was trying to establish common ground. He believed that "The overriding purpose of every plane, whether it is a bomber or a fighter, is to win the air battle on which final victory is predicated." Unfortunately, at that time his efforts fell on deaf ears, and the notion of indivisibility again went underground, only to resurface in the mid-1980s. It was put to rest in 1992 when the Air Force fused Strategic Air Command (SAC) and Tactical Air Command (TAC).

The importance of this event cannot be overstated. When we look at the air power team that fought in Operation Allied Force, we quickly discover that the

Chief of Staff Gen. Hoyt S. Vandenberg in 1951.

unity of effort airmen displayed might not have been possible if air power had continued along the great divide of strategic versus tactical air power.

This unity is expressed in doctrine, in strategy, in leadership, and in weapons systems. I am convinced that this notion of the indivisibility of air power was a major contributing factor to the success of air operations in Kosovo. Just look at the forces that participated in Allied Force. At our peak, we had nearly 1,100 aircraft from thirteen NATO nations supporting combat operations. Nearly two-thirds of the total were U.S. aircraft, contributed by the Air Force, Navy, Marine Corps, and Army, including unmanned aerial vehicles (UAVs), helicopters, air and sea launched cruise missiles, and carrier- and land-based air.

A statistic that affirms the sense of indivisibility is that of the total aircraft deployed only 535 were strike aircraft, of which the United States contributed 323. This means that less than half the aircraft were *shooters*. The remaining aircraft were *enablers*: air refueling assets; command and control platforms; and surveillance and reconnaissance platforms. Together with space and other C[4]ISR (command, control, communications, computer systems, intelligence, surveillance, and recon-naissance) assets, they contributed to a data fusion at the Combined Air Operations Center and put information where it was needed most—with the Joint Force Air Component Commander (JFACC) and his aircrews.

Looking at Allied Force, one thing becomes clear. Not only have we bridged the doctrinal divide within the Air Force but, from a joint perspective, airmen from all four services have made huge progress toward doctrinal cohesion. During Operation Allied Force, this created the conditions necessary for a diplo-matic solution, just as Billy Mitchell had predicted in 1925, when he wrote:

KC–135 accompanied by F–16Cs show how NATO's air forces controlled
the skies during operations over Serbia and Kosovo in 1999.

Air power holds out the hope...that...air battles taking place miles away from
the frontiers will be so decisive and of such far-reaching effect that the nation
losing them will be willing to capitulate without resorting to further contest
on land or water on account of the degree of destruction which would be sustained by the country subjected to...air attack.

We can only speculate on why Serbia's Slobodan Milosevic capitulated, but
Gen. Wesley Clark, the warfighting commander charged with executing military
operations, was unequivocal. He stated that "the air campaign empowered the
diplomacy and provided the incentives for Milosevic eventually to surrender."
Were he alive, I am sure Billy Mitchell would be with us tonight wearing an
"I told you so" grin!

Now, how is it that we, "empowered the diplomacy and provided the incentives for Milosevic eventually to surrender?" In aggregate, the Alliance flew
more than 37,000 sorties, with the United States contributing almost 25,000, or,
again, two-thirds. Of the 37,000 plus sorties, just over 9,500 were strike sorties
and, of those, U.S. airmen flew more than half. The results were telling.

As you all are aware, the Federal Republic of Yugoslavia had a robust
C^3(command, control, and communications) network. They learned from Iraq to
disperse, hide, and bury C^3 nodes. They also built in redundancies that made the
system even more resilient to include UK and U.S. radar systems—yes, even the
Westinghouse TPS–70.

Nevertheless, when we terminated Allied Force, their national C^3 operational
capability was degraded, despite the fact that they had spent the majority of their
national military treasure defending it. Some 30 percent of their radio relays
sustained moderate functional damage; 45 percent of their television broadcast
capability was severely degraded; their radio broadcast capability was limited to

F–16C taking off from Aviano Air Base, Italy, during Operation Allied Force.

urban areas; and Serb Socialist Party Headquarters and several other Alternate Command Posts sustained severe damage.

What about their air defense system? As with their C^3 network, the Federal Republic of Yugoslavia studied the Gulf War and designed their air defenses accordingly. They learned the value of mobile defenses and dispersed aircraft, and their tactics showed them to be astute students of Iraqi mistakes. Quite frankly, they were good, but not that good. We know we destroyed 35 percent of their MiG–21s; 85 percent of their MiG–29s; 66 percent of their SA–2 battalions; and 70 percent of their SA–3 battalions. An equally important target set, and a huge success story, was the work we did against the Serb defense industry. Strikes against this sector of the economy were designed to cripple the Serb army's ability to wage war and stifle their ability to conduct ethnic cleansing.

Along those lines, NATO air forces damaged or destroyed more than half of the Serb defense industry, including 40 percent of armored vehicle production; 50 percent of explosive production; 65 percent of ammunition production; 70 percent of aviation equipment assembly and repair; and 100 percent of petroleum refining. In addition, we effectively *owned* Serbia's electricity, turning it off, as required, to meet operational needs and to make it clear to Milosevic that he no longer controlled this essential facilitator of his military machine.

We also caused moderate damage to lines of communication country-wide. Over the Danube River we destroyed 70 percent of the road bridges; 50 percent of the rail bridges; and as a *collateral benefit* achieved total interruption of Danube River traffic. On the border with Montenegro, we completely halted rail traffic and degraded road traffic throughout. Along the Kosovo corridors, we cut 100 percent of the rail lines and interdicted 50 percent of road capacity. These numbers are impressive enough, but what is more impressive is that these targets were struck with precision. Throughout the operation, the United States released just under 24,000 weapons, of which 34 percent were precision munitions. It could be

B–1B from the 28th Bomber Wing at Royal Air Force Base Fairford, England.

argued, and analysis may ultimately prove, that the percentage was much higher. Maybe 70 to 80 percent of all targets were destroyed with precision munitions.

Consider this: B–1s and B–52s accounted for nearly half of all the weapons dropped by U.S. aircraft in Allied Force. A B–1 sortie with 84 Mk–82s, or a B–52 sortie with 45 Mk–82s each, could be targeted against just one desired point of impact. By contrast, a B–2 carrying 16 Joint Direct Attack Munitions (JDAMs), could be targeted against 16 different desired mean points of impact. That is a major shift in how we measure concentration of effort and mass. Of equal importance is the fact that the Joint Direct Attack Munition added a true all-weather capability.

Finally, airmen can strike targets any time, anywhere, day or night, in all-weather conditions. That is a significant addition to our nation's warfighting capability and marks a striking improvement from Desert Storm, where only 9 percent of the weapons were precision and of those a minute fraction, only 42 total weapons, were all-weather. Moreover, of the 42 weapons, 35 were Conventional Air Launched Cruise Missiles (CALCMs) and 7 Standoff Land Attack Missiles (SLAMs), using first-generation and preproduction Global Positioning System (GPS) guidance kits.

Given the apparent leap in precision capabilities we just witnessed in Allied Force, let us consider the implications of where we stand in the evolution of pre-cision warfare and how far we have come. Most laymen were introduced to the precision revolution during the Vietnam War, when video images of the destruc-tion of the Paul Doumer Bridge were broadcast on the evening news. At the time, the Paul Doumer was the longest and most important bridge in North Vietnam. Yet, its very size made it a relatively easy target even for *dumb bombs*.

F–4Cs dropping bombs over Vietnam.

But to airmen who flew in Vietnam, it was the destruction of the bridge at Than Hoa that made believers out of even the most ardent skeptics. Much harder to bring down because it was smaller and sturdier, the bridge at Than Hoa—called the Dragon's Jaw—was struck repeatedly between 1965 and 1968, without success. In 1965 alone, the Air Force and the Navy sent more than 800 sorties against the Dragon's Jaw and lost eleven aircraft in the process. In 1972, during Linebacker, Air Force F–4s dropped the Dragon's Jaw with twenty-four laser-guided bombs. For that era, this was a remarkable feat. It convinced our leaders to pursue a path toward precision that, by the time of the Gulf War, had transformed air power.

On *night one* of Desert Storm, attacks by strike aircraft and cruise missiles against air defense and command and control facilities opened up Iraq for subsequent conventional attackers. Precision attacks against the Iraqi air force destroyed it in its hangars and precipitated a bizarre attempt by Iraqi airmen to flee in their planes to Iran, their mortal enemy.

Equally instructive was how key precision weapon attacks against bridges served to *channel* the movement of Iraqi forces and create fatal bottlenecks. In previous conflicts, nonprecision interdiction efforts, such as the attack against the bridge at Than Hoa, took hundreds of sorties just to damage it. In the Gulf War, precision weapons quickly destroyed 41 of 54 key Iraqi bridges, as well as 31 hastily constructed pontoon bridges.

This is a far cry from how airmen defined precision in World War II. Indeed, it suggests precision may, in fact, be relative. Just one sampling of the precision daylight bombing of World War II confirms this. In 1944, it took 108 B–17 bombers, crewed by 1,080 airmen, dropping 648 bombs to guarantee a 96 percent

Courtesy of the History Office of the Italian Air Force.

Gen. Giulio Douhet.

chance of getting just two hits inside a German power-generation plant 400 feet by 500 feet. Contrast this to Allied Force, where a single strike aircraft, with two crew members, dropping one Joint Direct Attack Munition, could achieve the same results with a near-100 percent expectation of hitting the target. Clearly, precision warfare has come a very long way, and we have made great progress integrating precision capabilities into all four services.

If you look at the road we have traveled and project out into the future, you will likely discover that now that we have overcome the weather component of the combat equation, our next hurdle will be to overcome the time component. Giulio Douhet, in his 1921 dissertation on air power employment entitled *The Command of the Air,* wrote, "Victory smiles upon those who anticipate the changes in the character of war, not upon those who wait to adapt themselves after the changes occur."

As we move closer to the day when time becomes the decisive component in the character of war it is imperative we continue to master space, C^{4}ISR, precision, stealth, and information technologies, doctrine, and leadership. In the words of Sun Tzu, "a victorious army wins its victories before seeking battle."

Part V

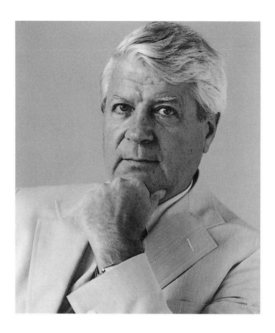

Admiral Train is currently manager, Hampton Roads Operations, Science Applications International Corporation (SAIC), a San Diego-based high technology research and development firm. He is also a senior fellow at the Joint and Combined Warfighting School, Armed Forces Staff College; and a mentor for the Institute for Defense Analyses's (IDA's) defense science studies group. Prior to his retirement from active duty in the U.S. Navy, Admiral Train served as NATO's Supreme Allied Commander, Atlantic; as Commander in Chief, U.S. Atlantic Command and as Commander in Chief, U.S. Atlantic Fleet. Other significant operational assignments have included command of the U.S. Sixth Fleet in the Mediterranean. His principal staff duties have included assignment as Director of the Joint Staff. Admiral Train is a 1949 graduate of the U.S. Naval Academy. In November 1998, he was appointed as a member of the Hart–Rudman Commission on National Security. This commission, set up under the aegis of the Secretary of Defense, Secretary of State, and National Security Advisor, is working to determine the global security environment of the first quarter of the twenty-first century; to analyze the character of the nation during that time frame and develop an appropriate national security strategy; and to recommend alternatives to the current national security apparatus and processes to implement the new strategy.

Information Superiority in Military Operations

Adm. Harry D. Train II, USN (Ret.)

Information superiority in military operations is hardly a new concept. Today, new technologies and new processes give it eminently added value, but the concept is as old as warfare itself. Those of you who might be familiar with the literary works of Patrick O'Brian and his series of historical novels about the Royal Navy during the Napoleonic Wars can recognize the application of information warfare in that comparatively primitive era. In O'Brian's partially historical plots, both information and misinformation were employed through the Royal Navy's intelligence apparatus, sometimes to extraordinary effectiveness.

Information warfare and information operations are the vehicles through which information superiority is attained. The highly technical character of information warfare today should not be allowed to mask the basic value of information superiority. A learned general officer colleague of mine frequently makes the point that there are always two parts of a battle: the battle for information and then the battle itself. In pursuing the battle for intelligence, the operators and intelligence folks today have far more effective tools at their disposal than did commanders in chief (CINCs) and their warfighting commanders back in my day. Today we enjoy enormous opportunity to leverage information warfare in ways that World War II commanders had never dreamed. When Admiral [Chester W.] Nimitz's cryptographers and operational staff faked an infrastructure breakdown on Midway Island, to test whether the Japanese code name for Midway had been correctly identified in intercepts, they were employing information warfare—the hard way. Whether it was pretty or not, it contributed to the defining victory of the Battle of the Pacific—Admiral [Raymond A.] Spruance's victory at the Battle of Midway. In the process, Spruance exploited information superiority.

The essence of war is not going to change, however. It is the technique of denial and deception that will lend itself to the exploitation of new technologies. The potential for nontraditional attack, created by the exploitation of new technologies, exposes new vulnerabilities. Information superiority implies that not only can we know more about the enemy than he knows about us, but also that we can defend our own information systems. Our military operations involve myriad computer-based control systems, high bandwidth communications links, and space-based intelligence and navigation systems, to name but a few. Electric power grids and transportation networks are as important to military operations

Fleet Admiral Chester W. Nimitz became Chief of Naval Operations
in December 1945.

as they are to the civilian infrastructure. The defense of computer networks, such
as these, is a crucially important dimension of information superiority. If the
enemy takes out the electric power grid of the mid-Atlantic states through cyber
attack, the Army is not going to move to its ports of embarkation. Strategic information warfare (SIW) is available to any adversary who chooses to employ
asymmetric warfare to compensate for his inability to face the balanced military
might of the United States directly. Successful cyber attacks against major
national command systems would function as a cheap means of immobilizing our
highly trained and well-equipped forces. Successful special forces or terrorist
attacks against key satellite ground control stations would neutralize space-based
systems that contribute to our own information superiority.

That these points are apparent to our national command authorities is evident
from the fact that our most recent Unified Command Plan revisions have
assigned the mission of computer network defense (CND) to CINCSPACE,
effective October 1, 1999. The mission will continue to be carried cut by the Joint
Task Force Computer Network Defense (JTF-CND).

Information superiority in military operations was a decisive factor in the Gulf
War. The British did not have information superiority in the Falkland Islands War,
but it did not matter because the Argentines did not have it either. We lacked it in
Somalia, and it did matter. In the case of Somalia it mattered because we thought
we enjoyed information superiority and operated as though we did. At the
beginning of the Mayaguez Crisis in 1975, we had zero information. Although
we gradually acquired information, as the four days of Mayaguez progressed,
we never came close to obtaining adequate information, much less information
superiority. Our casualty rate reflected this.

A C–130 delivers supplies during a humanitarian mission in Somalia.

A problem today is information overload and the concomitant difficulty of processing the large amount of information picked up through intelligence channels and distributed through the most efficient communication systems the world has ever seen. Even with the benefit of massively paralleled computer processing to help us sort out and understand that information, it requires quite a bit of skill on the part of decision makers to produce effective information and to use it as a force multiplier.

But there is a dimension of information warfare that is very sobering. The international aspects of U.S. business and commerce—including trade, transportation, telecommunications, investment, finance, and manufacturing—continue to expand. Because the health, welfare, and prosperity of American citizens depends upon computerized and information processing infrastructure, no nation in the world is more vulnerable or has more to lose than the United States. In information warfare defense we encounter not only the military dimension, but also the dimension of modern society. While strategic bombing of cities like London, Berlin, Tokyo, and Dresden that occurred during World War II is no longer a part of warfare, strategic information warfare has sprung fully armed from the brow of Zeus. This is in the form of asymmetric warfare, warfare waged by state or non-state actors who do not possess the full array of armed might enjoyed by the United States and her military allies. In effect, strategic information warfare is the use of weapons of mass disruption. States, terrorists, and other disaffected groups will likely acquire these cyber-war weapons of mass disruption and be in a position to use them. It is modern society, rather than the military, that is increasingly vulnerable.

Finally, we are experiencing some difficulty in employing the terminology of information warfare. When does information warfare stop being information warfare and become intelligence, or vice versa? What is the relationship between psychological operations and information warfare? Perhaps our other panelists will be able to shed some additional light on these and other aspects of this important topic.

General Hartzog retired from active duty in November 1998, after thirty-five years of distinguished service in the United States Army. His last assignment was as Commanding General, Training and Doctrine Command (TRADOC), Fort Monroe, Virginia, where his leadership and responsibility served TRADOC's mission by developing the Army's doctrine, training, and combat progression. From August 1993 to October 1994, he served as Deputy Commander in Chief and Chief of Staff of the United States Atlantic Command, Norfolk, Virginia. Previously, he was Commanding General, 1st Infantry Division at Fort Riley, Kansas; Commanding General, U.S. Army South, Fort Clayton, Panama; and J–3 for the United States Southern Command, Quarry Heights, Panama, during Operation Just Cause. General Hartzog also served as commander of the 197th Infantry Brigade and assistant commandant of the U.S. Army Infantry School at Fort Benning, Georgia. He was executive officer to the TRADOC Commanding General from June 1984 to September 1985. William Hartzog's earlier assignments include two tours in Vietnam and service as an instructor at the United States Military Academy, West Point, New York, from May 1969 to June 1972.

The Nintendo Generation

Gen. William W. Hartzog, USA (Ret.)

As a ground officer who has spent thirty-five years in the United States Army, I will try to share with you my experience in the tactical and operational aspects of information management and information warfare. Specifically, I will refer to a case study of the last four years of the Army's efforts in that regard. In doing so, I hope to get some lessons that can be extrapolated into the strategic business, and also discuss a few vulnerabilities and problems that are yet to be solved.

I became a commissioned officer in 1963. Later that year, I participated in a series of exercises in the eastern part of the United States called the Swift Strike Exercises. I had the interesting experience of walking into my first command post. It was in a series of tents; it was fairly large and very noisy; and it had the burble of radios in the background. People were running around drawing on acetate and overlaying flat paper maps on the walls. There was a ringmaster or two in the center shouting orders in an attempt to bring some order out of this business. That sounds an awful lot like every command post of any service you have ever been in.

Interestingly enough, in 1989 I was the operations officer for Just Cause in Panama. I was working for Gen. Max Thurman at the time. The command post was located in a tunnel, which might be the only difference between it and the 1963 command post. The Just Cause command post had radios, noise, some burble in the background, flat paper maps, and acetate symbology overlays.

Admiral [Harry] Train mentioned Haiti. In 1994 I was the deputy commander in chief (CINC) of the U.S. Atlantic Command and was in a command post in Norfolk, and there was a distinct difference. We had a lot of screens, it was much quieter, there were fewer maps, fewer people running around, and more centralization of information from both operational and tactical levels.

On the second day of that operation, the Marine Corps landed on the northern part of the island in a town called Cape Haitian. As they began to spread out and occupy a launchment area, a young lieutenant was leading a patrol down the main street of the town. Ten policemen, whose allegiance was unknown, were lounging on the front of a post office building, each armed with automatic weapons. As the Marine patrol walked past, they brought their automatic weapons up to the ready in a direct threat patrol, at which time the Marine patrol engaged them. The end result was that ten of the policemen were dead. A lieutenant who had never seen a day of combat in his life led the Marines.

C–130s lined up ready to assist during operations in Haiti.

As the report flashed up the chain of command as rapidly as digits and came into my ear, I was sitting next to the commander in chief. The CINC said "Get the lieutenant on the phone, I want to talk to him." I turned to the CINC and said "No, you don't" for a variety of reasons. But he said, "Yes, I do. I want to talk to him, and I want to talk to him right now." Interestingly enough, the technology allowed us to do that within about five minutes through telephone patches and satellite communications and other sorts of technology. When we contacted the lieutenant—whose name I am sorry to say I have forgotten—the admiral said, "Hey, lieutenant." I said "Sir, don't do this please," because I had visions of over-centralization and chain of command. The admiral continued, "Lieutenant, you did great," and hung up the phone. This was a super use of technology that could have been very bad for us.

So, a few seeds had begun to be planted. From 1994 to 1998, I had the privilege of being in charge of the Army's experimentation for future planning. And like General [Edward] Meyer before me, I was interested in the use of high technology so that we could use it rightly and not allow it to hamper or draw down some of the basics necessary to be successful in the business of war.

I want to talk a little bit about that case study, what those years brought us, where we are, and what we think we learned out of that. I will do it in terms of change, in terms of the challenge, some hypotheses with which we experimented, what we learned, what went wrong and right, and where we might go from here. I will try end with the linkage of the ground force picture and the other service capabilities that need to take us into full joint capability.

We started the process in 1994 with a lot of brain power, trying to figure out what we were looking at. We knew that there had been great changes in the world, all of the geographic, sociopolitical change that had occurred in 1989 and 1990, but we were also on the bow wave of a technological revolution that was running faster and faster—one that continues today. One of the first things that we did in 1994 was talk to a young man, who at the time not many folks understood or knew. His name was Bill Gates, and his people told us, "Whatever you do, understand that in the next few years we're going to come down to a hardware revolution every twelve to eighteen months and a software revolution every twelve months." They had undercut it by about 200 percent. I could not get to speak to him today, obviously, but he would tell you today that the software revolution is occurring within a month, and the hardware revolution is certainly something less than a year.

I am the proud owner of a 233 computer that I bought new for my son last year. He took it to college, wore it out, brought it home, and gave it back to me. I replaced it with a 600 capability computer, and that is not enough. The pace of change is one of the key factors in all this business, and the digestibility of what you see and what you think you know in response to it.

But in 1994 we began the process. The early thought business ranged all over the map: relative capabilities, countering information, how to sustain and manage information, horizontal distribution of information, individual mental capacity to accept information, overload—which we have already talked about that this morning—the right information at the right place at the right time—for what?

Well, after six months of this mental gymnastics, we boiled it down for the ground force at the tactical and operational level to three very simple hypotheses or three very central modes of thought. We felt that we could make a substantial increase in capability in all ways, sustainability, safety—all ways if we could answer three questions. If everyone in a ground force could answer accurately these questions: Where am I? Where are my subordinates? Where is the enemy? Now that is rather unsophisticated, but the answers to those questions are among the most complex considerations that I have ever been involved in.

During the four wars I participated in through my career, I rarely knew where I was specifically. In some of the wars, if you were in a foliated jungle environment, you never saw your subordinates except virtually. I did not know much about where the enemy was until I read it in the history books after the conflict. What would happen if you could do that in an organization that has a lot of moving parts? For example, an American ground division of some 15,000 people whom you want to get going in the same direction at the same time. Doctrine is a piece of it, thought is a piece of it, practice is everything, training is tremendous, but the pieces that we were always lacking were: Where am I? Where are my subordinates? And where is the enemy?

Fortunately, the Army agreed for me to take a test organization, it did not matter which one, and they gave me a budget. They told me to go out, take several years, and figure out how to do this. Well, I can report to you today that it is

B–52G taking off during the Gulf War, which demonstrated the importance
of the Global Positioning System in managing campaigns.

doable. And it is doable with a conglomeration of various kinds of technologies,
the Global Positioning System, satellite transmissions, and broadband broadcast-
ing. There were many more complex issues and developmental tasks that we did
than I have time to report on. But there is an organization in the Army today that
has the capability to answer those three things at each level most of the time.

What does it bring? It brings two things: (1) It brings mental agility in terms
of speed of operations, pace of decision making, and the ability to maneuver on
the ground that we have not had before. (2) It brings some knowledge, because
if you get the right information in the right place at the right time, then you can
have a great advantage over folks who are not similarly equipped.

At the same time there is a significant other side to that. It brings tremendous
challenges in leadership development. Do we have the right folks to use this sort
of technology? Can it be optimized? It brings challenges in vulnerabilities: If
someone steals the machine or captures the machine that gives you a picture of
the battlefield and updates in real time and feeds you a different picture, is it the
accurate picture or not? Then there is a panoply of similar kinds of technological
challenges. All I need to tell you is that there is such an organization with both
great benefits and some vulnerabilities.

Let me discuss a few of the lessons that were learned. On the first day of the
first exercise, after several years, we took this equipped, trained, and prepared
unit to a major exercise to test it. It was a brigade-sized element equipped and
trained with all this information technology, commanded by a very capable officer
who was forty-five years old at the time. He had been raised in an era that was
dominated by television. Most of my generation were raised in an era that started
with printed materials and audio signals from radios and went into the television
era. The younger members of this audience were raised in the Nintendo generation.

And here is what we found on the first morning of this exercise. Two minutes into the battle, the bugles had just blown, and the friendly force had moved out. Two minutes into the battle that particular commander, forty-five years old, had a 98 percent picture of where the enemy was, and what the enemy was doing. He had gotten it from the national reconnaissance satellites, plus the Joint Surveillance Target Attack Radar System (JSTARS), which provided moving target indicators. He had flown an unmanned aerial vehicle (UAV), and he had a look-down picture in movie quality of the enemy. He knew where 98 percent of the force was and could see what it was doing. Moreover, he had under his control long-range precise weapons and helicopter attack forces that had not been seen anywhere else in the world. He had tremendous capabilities. Do you know what he did? He sent out more reconnaissance patrols, more aircraft to validate what he thought he saw. Now, what was that all about? That is about a generation gap.

I did not understand that very well until 1996. At that time I had a seventeen-year-old son who was playing a high grade of hockey down in the Norfolk area, and he broke his back playing hockey. That accident gave me six months of quality time with my son. And he tried his very best to teach me how to play Nintendo and all the rest of those arcade games. At first I was convinced that my ineptness had something to do with eye-hand coordination, but it really did not.

Since that time I have had some scientists work on the problem. They found that what this forty-five-year-old commander experienced on the battlefield was the fact that he was raised to not trust or, said in a different way, to be skeptical of icons. Think about it. My generation was raised to ask things like "Is that really a battalion on that map?" "Is the enemy really flying that fast?" "I don't really believe that, that couldn't be, bring me some more intelligence." A part of the intelligence preparation of the battlefield is validating templates of what might be. Those who have been raised to play Nintendo find that the pace of the information flow is so great that if the first thirty seconds is spent in validating the template, one has lost the advantage. Therefore, we are at the cusp of this technological development that says the technologies have to be reliable, and they have to be good enough so that the icons can be trusted, or you lose the advantage of having them.

Now that is a terribly tough lesson. It makes you very skeptical, particularly if you are in charge of a project that is supposed to work. So, I started visiting elementary schools. A four-star general at an elementary school—it was interesting.

I wanted to find out if the youngsters who were going to man these systems and be our warriors of the future, whatever color their uniforms, in the 2020 to 2025 time frame, were being raised in sufficiently different ways to overcome this generation gap, without some specific training experience on our part.

The first school I visited was in Mantua, out toward Fairfax, Virginia. A sixth grader gave me a very lucid presentation on the inner workings and hidden mechanisms of an oscilloscope. I own an oscilloscope because I play with an old car, but I could not tell you how it works. You turn on the switch and it lights up, telling you whether or not it works. But this sixth grader knew. He gave me a computerized presentation. Actually, the boy did not care about the computer because he had covered the technologies and the computer four years earlier. He was focused only on the subject.

If that is an indicator—and I have found it validated in many other places—then we will be fine. We do not need a private in the Army, a yeoman, an airman with twenty-five hours of college-level technology before they come into the 2020 force. The other piece that I think we learned in all of this process is vulnerability. As I was working through the funding in the aftermath of this four-year study, I had to visit Sen. John Glenn on the Hill many times. I had to convince Senator Glenn that this was worthy of his support, right committee, right place. I was a little bit apprehensive about that. Trying to brief John Glenn on technology just did not seem right to me because of my age and what he had done in life. But he was very supportive of the process and the effort. Yet, every day I had to go through about forty minutes' worth of vulnerabilities. And the forty minutes' worth of vulnerabilities were not what the enemy was going to preclude us from doing with this system that told you where you were and where your subordinates were and where the enemy was. Rather, it had to do with what we would do to ourselves. His attitude was born of his personal experience of how very difficult it was to make technology work. We are a long way from having all of these technologies be simplistic enough to be hands off. There are still men and women in the loop every day, with all of the fragilities and vulnerabilities that come with punching the wrong button.

I work with a subcommittee at the same National Security Study Group that Admiral Train mentioned earlier. After the roll out, I was going to give a summary of all that experience to the chief of staff of the Army, who had asked me how it went. I typed out an e-mail, my little finger of the right hand slipped, I beamed it into the stratosphere; and I wasted an hour in doing it yesterday morning. I brought in three experts in the company that I run and had them teach me what not to touch. I did it all again, touched another button, and sent it to my secretary, who sits on the other side of the door. I learned a long time ago that maybe we are our own worst enemies in using the technology, and that leadership and technological developments are required.

In summary, I had the great privilege and opportunity to walk on the cusp of new technologies and explore how they might be useful in, at least, one dimension of our national defense. In the process, I learned that we are finished with the beginning. We are not really afraid of the process, but the beginning is the lower left-hand corner of a very large box. These technologies are not being developed in a coherent joint way today. It was like shoving a noodle up a hill.

Some Air Force friends and I in this experimentation business got together, and we concluded that it would be nice if every pilot who flew over a battlefield was interested in what was happening on the ground, and if everyone on the ground who was sitting under the descending bombs and munitions from the plane had the same picture of what was going on. It would be nice, we all agreed. Certainly the technology is there, but that is just the beginning; we have just started to learn. Because this beautifully colored picture that the ground commander needs, including the icons that he can eventually learn how to use to his benefit, is totally useless to a pilot who is flying at mach X who only has time, among all the other things that he or she is doing, to drink in Xs and Os. Therefore, he or she works in a John Madden [football commentator] language while the folks on the ground have a different picture.

Is that being done today? I do not think so. If it is, I cannot put my hands on it. Does it need to be happening? Yes, I think so. It has to be part of our culture that we have a common language. How do we get that done? I have some ideas about all that, but it is there to be done.

After graduating from the United States Military Academy at West Point in 1950, Lincoln Faurer entered pilot training and embarked on a thirty-five-year career in the Air Force. The early years were spent flying B–29s in both the Strategic Air Command (SAC) and Air Weather Service (AWS). In the latter duty, he served in Japan, supporting the war in Korea, and searching for and fixing the location of typhoons. After his return to the United States, he attended Navigator-Bombardier School, so that he could join the ranks of triple-rated SAC pilots flying B–47s. Then came headquarters staff duty, preparing launch crews to cope with the first several models of intercontinental ballistic missiles (ICBMs). After earning a master's degree in engineering management from Rensselaer Polytechnic Institute, he began his exposure to the intelligence field at the Defense Intelligence Agency (DIA). Subsequently, he attended the National War College and earned a master's degree in international relations from the George Washington University. General Faurer then embarked on a string of senior assignments that included J–2 at SOUTHCOM, Deputy Assistant Chief of Staff for Intelligence (ACSI), Vice Director of DIA, J–2 EUCOM, Deputy Chairman of the NATO Military Committee, and Director of the National Security Agency (NSA), from which he retired in 1985. From 1986 to 1991 he was the president and CEO, Corporation for Open Systems, an R&D firm responding to a consortium of communications and computer vendor and user companies seeking to accelerate a world-wide "open systems" environment. Presently, he provides consulting services on intelligence issues and serves as a volunteer in a number of intelligence associations and organizations.

Intelligence Support to the Warfighter*

Lt. Gen. Lincoln D. Faurer, USAF (Ret.)

Background

Although good intelligence has always been indispensable to successful oper-ations, the historically-uneasy marriage of intelligence and operations continues to the present. In this paper, I will be speaking of intelligence as it applies to mil-itary operations and the decisions implicit in the same. I embrace in the function of intelligence the tasking, collection, processing, exploitation, and dissemination (TCPED) of intelligence, surveillance, and reconnaissance (ISR) assets employing all disciplines.

History clearly establishes the need of the commander for knowledge of the battlespace, that is, timely intelligence support, in order to outmaneuver the enemy. Today we refer to the need to be within the enemy's OODA [observe, ori-ent, decide, and act] loop. Much effort by operators and intelligence folks has always gone into stating operational requirements for "Intel" satisfaction. Nevertheless, the relationship between the two camps has been more one of an arm's-length interaction than a harmonious integration. Intel is reluctant to fully divulge capabilities and even—in many instances—information for fear of com-promising and losing capabilities. The situation has been highlighted by the "Green Door" compartmentation and exclusion. At the outset of Desert Storm, command and staff level understanding of satellite reconnaissance capabilities and constraints was negligible. It had been highly compartmented and was not shared outside of selected intelligence circles.

On the other hand, operators and commanders have been secretive with respect to planning and reluctant to share specific intentions for similar fears of compromise. This is a situation aggravated by the "Black Door." I can tell you from firsthand experience that in the planning for Grenada, for example, the National Security Agency (NSA) was not informed and, hence, was precluded from making the necessary preparations to reconfigure assets and determine a signals intelligence background.

---

* Much of the material for this paper is based on a "Finding and Recommendation of the Intelligence and Vigilance Panel of a 1999 Air Force Scientific Advisory Board Summer Study Concerning Operations Other Than Conventional War (OOTCW)."

Today:
Separated, Serial, Unsynchronized
TCPED/Operational Cycles

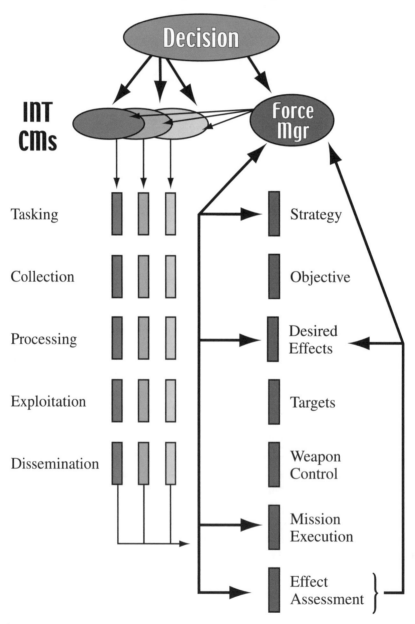

Figure 1

The Goal:
Collaborative, Synchronized Decision Environment

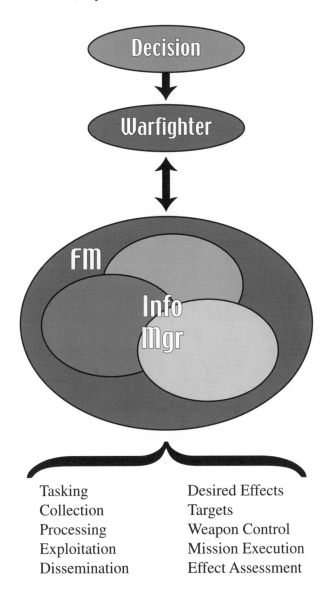

Tasking   Desired Effects
Collection   Targets
Processing   Weapon Control
Exploitation   Mission Execution
Dissemination   Effect Assessment

**JOINT BATTLESPACE INFOSPHERE
GLOBAL GRID**

Figure 2

The result of the aforementioned attitudes is that we have two autonomous processes that interface in less than an optimal fashion. To fully appreciate the extent of the problem, we must remind ourselves that an optimal interface between intelligence and operations really must occur within the broad context of information. Henceforth, I will address the shortcomings of Intel operating in support of the warfighter, within the context of optimized information management.

Today

The current Intel cycle—TCPED—is sequential, oriented toward particular systems and security compartments, and isolated from the command and control environment. (See Fig. 1) During the Cold War, with the world in a bipolar state, this approach was a significant component of the "big win" philosophy. For the foreseeable future, however, U.S. forces will often deploy rapidly to areas where little *a priori* information is available about the threat environment, civilian disposition, leadership intentions, and infrastructure. Operations within the past decade serve as examples of the shortfalls of the current modes of interaction between ISR and operations for many of the missions that will confront the United States in the future. ISR information was prepared based on the assumptions of the ISR details, in a non-time coincident manner. As a result, information critical to operational success was often placed in the hands of the warfighter out of "synch" with the operation. Many of the delays were associated with the asynchronous, compartmented, separate management of the force structure and ISR assets. This was further exacerbated by the lack of an interoperable information infrastructure and communications network. In the end, commanders were forced into action without full benefits of our current technology. Lessons from such operations, combined with yet additional advances in technology, suggest a concept where ISR and force management are *integral* to each other— not just *interoperable*—and stand on a consistent information infrastructure, communications, and network foundation.

Tomorrow

The future requires levels of responsiveness and agility in the acquisition, assimilation, and delivery of information that are inconsistent with rigid cycle structures and demand, instead, a framework that is intrinsically dynamic. (See Fig. 2) Arguably, a shift from the traditional ISR cycle to an information system that is responsive to the new intelligence warfighter is mandatory if the Expeditionary Aerospace Force (EAF) is to succeed. Indeed, in an ideal system of the future, the integrated ISR-C^2 information management system (IMS) process should be a fully integrated component of the command and control system. From the warfighter's point of view, the specification of a commanded action—ranging from mission definition, to course of action specification, to the issuing of an air tasking order (ATO), to effects assessment—has associated with

M1 Abrams tank, guided by the Global Positioning System, crosses a minefield
during Desert Storm.

it clearly identifiable information needs to which the IMS process should respond automatically and effectively. A useful analogy is to think in terms of the "handling qualities" of the IMS process. When an information need is presented to the information management process, the fulfillment of that need should appear to be as direct and easily controlled as the direct tasking of a specific asset that is "owned" by the warfighter.

The warfighter must have the information available in a timely and "tailorable" manner, assured through a structured process and infrastructure. Comprehensive, dynamic, and almost real-time knowledge bases, about the diverse threat areas, with an ability to refresh rapidly, must be available to the warfighters. This requires that the loop from the decision maker through to the shooter be empowered by current and future technology, in a manner that the knowledge and information base is current, accredited, and readily available. The goal must be to create and deploy a collaborative, synchronized decision environment for the warfighter, making the IMS and battle management processes integral elements of the same overall system.

To achieve this goal requires both major cultural and structural changes and significant technology development. It requires determining to design "process" to meet the future and have the desirable process lead the development of technology. Too often we have tended to wait for technology development to nudge us in the direction of better processes. The penalty for doing so is tardiness in readying for the future. The "better IMS process" depicted in this chart involves a completely integrated, collaborative environment, with information needs dynamically defined in response to the evolving military situation and the needs of the new *Information Warfighter.*

Relevant Technologies

I will not go very deeply into the technology development essential to achieving an IMS integrated into battle management, but will identify the areas in which effort is required and where advanced work is underway. This work comes under five major headings: Representation of Information, Information Fusion, Dynamic Allocation of Assets, Interaction with the User, and Performance Assessment.

Representation of Information: The design of the data structures to be used for the IMS is a challenging problem for at least four significant reasons.

(1) The structure must be capable of dealing seamlessly with the high-dimensionality, heterogeneity, and multiple granularities of the information provided directly by the full suite of ISR resources or required as information products by users of the IMS.

(2) The representation must facilitate the assimilation of data from a wide variety of sources, each of which provides quite different "apertures" into the information space.

(3) The design of data structures for the IMS to deal with the user must cope with the serious challenge to develop data structures that support military information needs.

(4) The information representation must be designed to anticipate the nature and character of information, collected or requested, that will evolve as new sensing technologies are developed and new types of contingencies are encountered.

Information Fusion: The fundamental challenge is to develop an information fusion architecture and associated algorithms that can deal effectively with the complexity of reasoning and fusing information over space, time, and hierarchy. This must be done in a manner that exploits and exposes the structure of military situations and is guaranteed to produce products that are better than any of the constituent materials on which they are based.

Dynamic Allocation of Assets: Our future system requires the warfighter to have virtual control over, rather than rigid ownership of, specific sensing assets, with the IMS serving as the mediator and scheduler of a suite of assets to meet the combined needs of all its users. This implies the need to develop large-scale dynamic resource allocation algorithms, capable of dealing with dimensionality and complexity that matches that of the information fusion function.

Interaction with the User: Different warfighters will have differing information needs. The information query system required must allow the user to request precisely the information needed, but to do so implicitly by identifying the purpose. For example, think of the IMS as an embedded system within a command and control system, that is, as a component of a very large and complex servo loop. The query might be simply the statement of a particular mission, with the embedded information needs implicit in the mission statement. When an air tasking order is specified, an entire sequence of information needs can be defined, including when each piece of information is needed: for example, enemy activities along the flight path, threatening surface-to air missile (SAM) locations, detailed target-related information, and bomb damage assessment (BDA) information after ATO completion. The query system must also allow for specialized queries related to particular contingencies that require exceptionally fast response cycles. Short circuiting some information digestion may be required to expedite a sensor-to-shooter loop. In turn, that will necessitate use of decision theory to address the tradeoff between delay in action and false detection.

Another important characteristic to be incorporated into the query structure is user drill-down into the database. Normally, the IMS will be fused products of direct use to the decision maker, with minimal extraneous detail or clutter. However, the user must be able to drill down into the IMS to view the raw materials that produced a fused product.

A technology area at a very early stage of development that holds great promise for many of these issues—it is finding use on the Internet—is that of intelligence agents. We can imagine the development of algorithms that allow agents to learn the critical elements of the user's decision space and then to use this knowledge to generate an information need profile. It is, at this point, a vision rather than a reality, but it does represent a very attractive vision whose realization should be part of the technology investment strategy.

Performance Assessment: It is important that the development of the IMS for command and control be coupled with development of measures of performance (MOPs) and the means for their evaluation. The IMS needs MOPs for its own operation, e.g., quantifying the performance of the fusion process, and performance models for the dynamic resource scheduler. Developing MOPs will not be an easy task and will need more attention than performance assessment has received historically.

Summary

I hope that the Air Force will urge and lead Department of Defense (DoD) efforts to attain a "real-time" intelligence and knowledge-based environment, integral with battle management activities. (See Fig 2). Of course, to effect a change of this magnitude will require significant technology development, as well as cultural and structural changes, and consequently must take shape over an extended period. Frankly, the easier half of the solution may lie on the technology side. Although much of the needed development may be little more presently than conceptualizing by technologists, determined collaboration among the services, industry, and academia would likely meet, in time, all the needs I have discussed in the five technology areas. On the other hand, effecting cultural and structural changes, particularly in the intelligence community, will take determined and enlightened senior leadership at the agencies and within the services.

If my assertion is correct—that the nature of future force employment demands responsive information management better coupled with command and control—an Air Force commitment to lead change toward the collaborative, synchronized decision environment, should be a "no-brainer."

Part VI

General Meyer graduated from the United States Military Academy in 1951 and earned an MS degree from the George Washington University in 1967. He also graduated from the Command and General Staff College, the Armed Forces Staff College, and the National War College. He served as a rifle company commander and a battalion staff officer through three major campaigns in the Korean conflict. During the Vietnam War, he served with the 1st Cavalry Division as a battalion commander, brigade commander, and division chief of staff. After duty as assistant division commander with the 82d Airborne Division and deputy commandant of the Army War College, he commanded the 3d Infantry Division in Germany. He was the Deputy for Operations and Plans on the Army General staff from 1976 to 1979, and from 1979 until his retirement in 1983, was Chief of Staff, U.S. Army, and a member of the Joint Chiefs of Staff. Since retirement, he has served on the President's Strategic Defense Initiative Panel, the Defense Science Board, and other governmental advisory boards and panels. He is a member of the board of directors of ITT Industries, AEGON USA, and Mitretek Systems. He is a member of the board of governors of the Smith Richardson Foundation, the Board of Overseers of the Hoover Institution, the Trustees of the George Marshall Foundation, and the Board of Advisors of CSIS. Currently, he is Chairman of Mitretek Systems, Managing Partner of Cilluffo Associates L. P., and President of Army Emergency Relief.

Strategic Imperatives

Gen. Edward C. Meyer, USA (Ret)

Over the past fifty years, the United States Air Force has become a first-line player in the national security arena. It plays a vital role across the full spectrum of warfare, from peacekeeping, to limited wars, to nuclear deterrence. A review of history permits one to develop certain strategic imperatives that must be observed if we are to be prepared for the twenty-first century and its many uncertainties. Our national security strategy must continue to be that of the survival of our nation—a nation that will continue to observe the promises contained in the United States Constitution and in our Bill of Rights.

One must be careful in defining imperatives. I have chosen to define them as threats to our survival, our way of life, and our prosperity. Those are my imperatives. I will look at ten conditions that exist today that I believe could have a negative impact on our way of life, if they are not addressed urgently.

Imperative 1: Russian Nuclear, Chemical, and Biological Weapons

While some might argue about whether Russia will remain a single nation or break up into three or four separate nations, the real threat to our survival are the weapons of mass destruction that Russia possesses. Therefore, getting rid of the Russian nuclear weapons as a threat is a national strategic imperative of the first order. The Nunn-Lugar initiative and efforts by former Secretary of Defense William J. Perry are aimed to address this threat. However, despite these and other efforts, progress has been slow. It is imperative that we get on with the destruction of these weapons as rapidly as possible. To accomplish this will require agreement on several nuclear-related issues. Nonetheless, the sooner we can get rid of the massive number of weapons and amounts of nuclear materials in the hands of the Russians, the sooner we can begin to ensure the survival of our way of life into the twenty-first century.

Imperative 2: China

In the twenty-first century, China has the potential to become a major strategic player in the international arena. Our goal must be to assist China in growing as a responsible member of the world community. While China's capabilities today cannot seriously threaten our way of life, we must establish policies that attempt to align China with our own goals for the future. This means that we

Crewmen prepare the A–10 for a mission in the Middle East.

must maintain as much contact and leverage as possible with China. One major consideration in this relationship involves the future of Taiwan. We must make clear to the leaders of the People's Republic of China that a military attack on Taiwan would involve the United States in the conflict. We must also make it clear to both parties that we favor a long-term solution to their differences, preferably through interactions between the two entities. A competitive China in the future should be acceptable, as long as the competition does not threaten our survival.

Imperative 3: Mexico

I am not off my rocker and do not expect an armed Mexico to attack us from the south.This imperative serves to remind us that our way of life is subject to attacks other than military. Social and economic threats exist as well. Consider what might happen if the Mexican economy were to go under. What control would be needed to manage population migration, increased illegal drug traffic, and the myriad challenges posed by a nation on our border beset by serious economic straits? Mexico raises the importance of the Americas to the United States. We must become more serious about the nations to our south, from Mexico to Argentina to Chile. The economic potential of the Americas may have a significant impact on our way of life.

Imperative 4: Europe

This item clearly is not intended to imply isolationism. We must remain an active member of the Atlantic Alliance. However, the United States does not need to lead it for the next one hundred years. Projections for the populations and economies of the current members of the European Union indicate that in a decade or so they will be equivalent to those of the United States. While our goal should be to ensure the continuation of the Atlantic Alliance, we need not be so wedded to the past that we are precluded from developing new relationships that reflect more accurately the capabilities of all parties concerned. Needless to say, there are many European issues that will require less and less U.S. involvement.

Imperative 5: The Middle East

In the twenty-first century, it is imperative that we reduce our dependence on Middle Eastern oil. We should not be dragged into another war on account of oil. Our relationships with Israel, Egypt, Saudi Arabia, and other Middle Eastern countries should continue as long as Iraq and Iran pose threats to our friends in the region. However, our reliance on oil from the Middle East can certainly be offset by greater efforts in other geographically uncontested oil-producing areas. We should also address the technological alternatives to oil that could improve and protect our environment.

Imperative 6: Space

Our nation and our military are totally dependent upon space assets. Today, space assets provide communications and relays, intelligence gathering, position locating, business, finance, medical, and myriad other daily needs. Without these space assets, many of our military systems would have difficulty operating. Securing our space assets and ensuring that they are available will be a major requirement for the twenty-first century. The United States Space Command will play an ever-increasing role in this vital area.

Imperative 7: Homeland Defense

Much is being said and written today about the importance of homeland defense. The threats that exist to our society from weapons of mass destruction, cyber warfare, and other means by which future enemies can bring destruction and terror to our homeland continue to grow. In that context, there are many legal, institutional, and bureaucratic issues that must be addressed and resolved. However, if we cannot provide security for our cities and towns, the very nature of our society will be threatened. Some of the critical issues to be faced that relate to the military are the roles of the National Guard, the Reserves, and Space Command.

Imperative 8: National Security Strategy

As the next century arrives, it is crucial that we develop a national security strategy and the resources to support it to deal with the world's political, economic, military, and environmental changes. This strategy must consider the first seven imperatives. Moreover, this strategy must be addressed by all elements of our government that are concerned with the basic survival of our way of life as envisaged by America's founding fathers. Today, our basic values are under attack

The F–117 Stealth fighter exemplifies the evolving technology on which
national security depends.

and they will continue to be threatened into the next century. It is vital to develop
a new national security strategy and concomitant policies to protect our way of
life and ensure our prosperity.

Imperative 9: Manning the Force

A previous panel addressed the challenges in enlisting and retaining the quality men and women required to ensure that our armed forces remain capable of
responding to threats to our survival. While not relating directly to that panel, one
area needs special emphasis. Personnel policies and offices deal with individuals, while military forces train and fight as units. For those services that require
rapidly deployable, cohesive units, the personnel systems have to be reordered to
make certain that cohesive units are central to their policies.

Imperative 10: Equipping the Force

If we are to ensure that we have technological superiority on any future battlefield—from earth to space—we must be willing to invest sufficiently to ensure
that we are never second best in any future conflict. A previous panel discussed
the technology issues in significant depth. The watchword for our future is not to
permit our forces to be at a disadvantage technologically. To achieve this will
require constant resources for research, development, and testing. We owe our
servicemen and women nothing less.

Conclusion

The imperatives outlined above are those that must be addressed in the first five years of the new millennium if we are to ensure that the words of a sage strategist of the twentieth century are to be realized. When asked what our national security policy ought to be, he replied, "To survive, perhaps to prosper." I hope that we can at least do that.

Glossary

ACSI	assistant chief of staff for intelligence
AEF	Aerospace Expeditionary Force
AIDS	Acquired Immune Deficiency Syndrome
AMRAAM	advanced medium-range air-to-air missile (AIM-120)
ATO	air tasking order
AWS	Amphibious Warfare School
AWS	Air Weather Service
BDA	bomb damage assessment
C^3	command, control, and communications
C^4ISR	command, control, communications, computer systems, intelligence, surveillance, and reconnaissance
CAIV	cost as an independent variable
CALCM	conventional air-launched cruise missile
CCSS	Command and Control Systems School
CIA	Central Intelligence Agency
CINC	commander in chief
CINCPAC	Commander in Chief, Pacific
CIPE	Center for International Political Economy
CND	computer network defense
CNO	chief of naval operations
COTS	commercial off-the-shelf software
CSC	Command and Staff College
CSIS	Center of Strategic and International Studies
DCS/R&D	deputy chief of staff for research and development
DIA	Defense Intelligence Agency
DoD	Department of Defense
EAF	Expeditionary Air Force
EO	electro-optical
EU	European Union

EUCOM	European Command
FAR	Federal Acquisition Regulation
FARA	Federal Acquisition Reform Act
FASA	Federal Acquisition Streamlining Act
FMF	Fleet Marine Force
GPS	Global Positioning System
GUI	graphic user interface
ICBM	intercontinental ballistic missile
IDA	Institute for Defense Analyses
IFOR	Implementation Force
IMS	information management system
ISR	intelligence, surveillance, and reconnaissance
IT	information technology
JCS	Joint Chiefs of Staff
JDAM	Joint Direct Attack Munition
JFACC	Joint Forces Air Component Commander
JFS	Joint Strike Fighter
JSTARS	Joint Surveillance Target Attack Radar System
JTF-CND	Joint Task Force Computer Network Defense
MACV	Military Advisory Command, Vietnam
MAGTF	Marine Air-Ground Task Force
MCU	Marine Corps University
MCWAR	Marine Corps War College
MOP	measure of performance
NASA	National Aeronautics and Space Administration
NATO	North Atlantic Treaty Organization
NCO	noncommissioned officer
NIPRNET	Non-secure Internet Protocol Router Network
NRO	National Reconnaissance Office
NSA	National Security Agency
OCS	Officer Candidate School

OODA loop	observe, orient, decide, and act loop
OOTCW	operations other than conventional war
PEO	program executive officer
PJE	professional joint education
PME	professional military education
POW	prisoner of war
RAF	Royal Air Force
R&D	research and development
RDJTF	Rapid Deployment Joint Task Force
RDT&E	research, development, test and evaluation
ROTC	Reserve Officer Training Corps
SAC	Strategic Air Command
SAIC	Science Applications International Corporation
SAM	surface-to-air missile
SAT	standardized aptitude test
SAW	School of Advanced Warfighting
SHAPE	Supreme Headquarters Allied Powers Europe
SIPRNET	Secure Internet Protocol Router Network
SIW	strategic information warfare
SLAM	Standoff Land Attack Missile
SNCO	staff noncommissioned officer
TAC	Tactical Air Command
TBS	The Basic School
TCPED	tasking, collection, processing, exploitation, and dissemination
TRADOC	Training and Doctrine Command
UAV	unmanned aerial vehicle